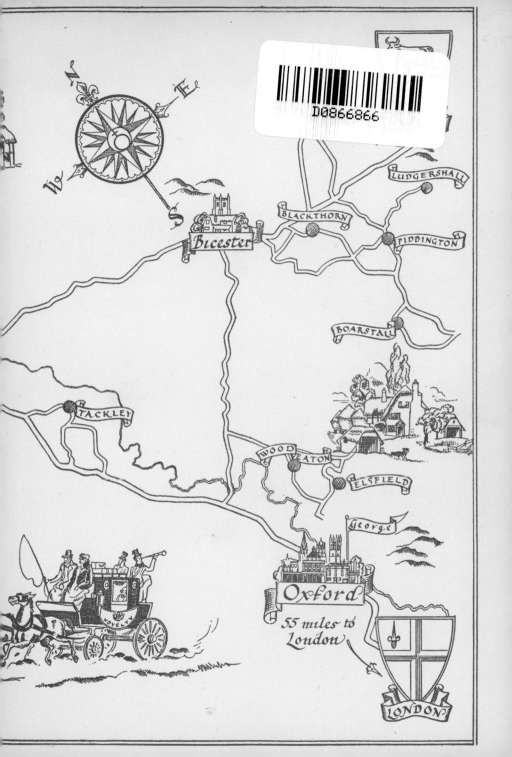

# INHERITANCE

Reconstructs everyday life in
England of 18th Century.

(ad - N.Y. Times Book Rev., Nov. 15, 1931, p.10)

A Portrait Bust of John Drinkwater by Sava Botzaris

# INHERITANCE

BY

JOHN DRINKWATER

NEW YORK

HENRY HOLT AND COMPANY

# ILLUSTRATIONS

# INHERITANCE

# I

OF the years before nine, I remember almost nothing. When I was still in frocks, I went to stay with my grandfather at Oxford. An unpleasant person in his household offended me. One morning, while she was dressing me in a starched white frock that stuck out round me like a diminutive ballet skirt, she was more offensive than usual. When I was clothed, she left me, and with bad thoughts I went downstairs. There I found another person, on her knees, scrubbing the floor. Beside her was a pail, into which she wrung her dirty cloth; it was full of black bubbling water. Silently, and with malice in my heart, I watched until her eyes were turned, then sat squarely in the pail, taking the starch out of my frock, and, I evilly hoped, out of my oppressor.

When I was a little older, I suppose six or thereabouts, an alarming thing happened to me. Each night in bed I went through a ritual with my Mother. She had to promise me in turn that neither a lion, nor a tiger, nor a bear, nor a wolf would come into the room when she had gone away. Outside the house there used to be a frightening noise which I was told was a German band. My bedroom window was high up in the wall behind my bed, too high for me to look out of it. One night I heard the noise out in the street, and then another scraping noise on the wall outside my window. In terror I looked up, and there was the German band staring in at me in the dark. It was like a wolf with a square head. I was told that it was a cat that had come along a ledge; but I have never liked German bands since.

I can only remember one toy. It was a horse-race game, with a board that took up the whole of a table, with hedges and ditches, and a box-wood cup with dice in it. When I was old enough, I went to a dame's school somewhere in Ladbroke Grove, kept by a Mrs. Zinck. It backed on to the common gardens of a square, and at eleven each morning we went out to walk round a circular gravel path enclosing a bed of shrubs and lilac bushes. If you had no lunch of your own, the establishment gave you a slice of dry bread, and I used to eat this in the solemn companionship of a leggy little girl who wore a tartan skirt. Her home was near to mine, and we used to walk to and from school together, until my Father said that it was muffish not to walk with a boy. Mrs. Zinck's bombazine dress, and the bread-slices, and the round walk, and the little girl

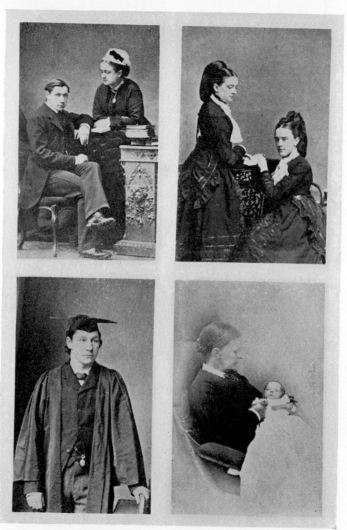

The author's father and mother; his mother and her
sister; his father; and the author, himself.

in tartan are all that I can remember of my first school.

We were then living in a crescent that has since been absorbed by the slum that had already crept up to it. We had the second floor of a house, and my only playground was the street. Here I was allowed to amuse myself as I liked, with strict orders that on no account was I to enter the forbidden territory beyond. One day I was playing with a small hard rubber ball, painted red, which cost a penny. Kicking it too hard, I saw it roll over the boundary line, where an errand-boy picked it up. As he made off with it, I shouted to him to give it back, and he pulled a long nose at me. I started in pursuit, and then remembered my orders. It would, I know, have been more dashing to forget them, but there it is. Clenching my hands and standing with my toes on the frontier kerb-stone, I watched the thief disappear into darker London. From that moment I was in revolt against all unreasonable rules. It took me a good many years to learn better.

When I was born at Leytonstone in Essex, my Father was a master at Coburn Foundation School. He was supposed to be doing very well, and when he took to the stage there was consternation in the family. Membership of an amateur society called The Glow-worms had been tolerated, but there was something dangerous about a professional actor. To me it was very exciting. I had a great admiration for him, because he could lift me off the ground as I hung on to a walking-stick that he held by the ends, which seemed a feat of incredible strength. And then he used to bring people to the house to rehearse plays, and one of them whose part made no great demands on his time took me to a Naval and Military Exhibition, where I saw a sea-fight between miniature men-of-war. Once, in my own opinion, I became famous. In those days, copyright in a play was secured by a fictitious performance. It had to be advertised for production at a theatre or licensed hall, and money had to be taken. One bill used to be printed and placed on view, and tickets were priced at five pounds or so each. On the appointed day a company assembled, a friend who had been provided with five pounds bought a ticket at the box-office, and the play was read from the stage. On one such occasion, when a play of my Father's was to be copyrighted an actor defaulted and I took his place, reading my part from a carefully written manuscript bound in brown paper. I knew nothing about the play, and as my book contained only my own part and cues of two or three words underlined in red ink, I was very anxious as I waited with my finger on the cue that would tell me when next to speak. The play was called *A Golden Sorrow*, and the following day I wrote one myself, called *Sorrow Turned Into Joy*. This had eleven acts, and lasted about seven minutes.

Still under nine, I used to be taken by my Father on tour, as there was no convenient place to leave me, my Mother being already an invalid. He was in a Shakespearean and Old English Comedy company, and he used to share lodgings with three other actors, one of whom was Lyall Swete. I still have a book, *Rumplestiltskin and Other Plays*, given to 'Jack from Ted with love and New Year wishes. 1890.' These four actors were all playing important parts, Bassanios and Joseph Surfaces and Mr. Hardcastles and Trinculos, and their salaries, which they pooled for housekeeping, amounted to five pounds a week between them. I was not often allowed to go with them to the theatre, being put to bed before they left, though I remember watching my Father acting Antonio in *The Merchant of Venice* when an act drop fell on his head and I thought he was killed. But rushing round to the back of the stage I heard him talking to a scene-shifter in a way which showed he wasn't.

On one tour the company had a cricket eleven, and I was included to field long-stop, a place unknown to the higher circles of the game. But it was

[ 7 ]

extremely agitating, as we had what seemed to me a very fast bowler, and my Father, who kept wicket, allowed a large number of deliveries to escape him. My duty being to save boundaries, and the outfield usually being virgin soil, orthodox fielding was ineffective, and I learnt how to charge the uncertain ball and throw myself upon it with great precision. As I played in flannel knickers and bare knees I acquired many honourable scars in the service. I suppose I was on the batting list, but I do not remember ever going in.

A. E. Drinkwater in J. H. Leigh's production of *The Tempest*, at the Court Theatre; from the *Sporting and Dramatic News*.

## II

At the age of nine I was sent to school at Oxford, where I was to live with my Grandfather. I remember my Mother's distress when I went away; it was the last time I saw her, she dying soon afterwards. I travelled alone, and by some mistake there was no one to meet me at Oxford station. After wondering for a few minutes what to do, I got into a cab and told the driver to take me to my Grandfather's house. When I arrived, I rang the front door bell, and told the maid that there was the fare to pay. My Uncle Charles was in the hall, and I heard him say something about a young cub. After that I was always a little afraid of him, but I came to like him, and he was often friendly to me in the years that followed.

My Grandfather, John Beck Brown, my Mother's father, was an ironmonger in Cornmarket, and his house was in Winchester Road. All his brothers were Oxfordshire or Buckinghamshire farmers, and he had set up business with a good connection in agricultural implements. He was already a very imposing old man, a full six feet tall, with masses of quite white curly hair. I lived with him for five years, until he died, and I never had a cross word from him. On weekdays I only saw him in the evening, when before going to bed each night I played one game of bezique or a rubber of cribbage with him. Sometimes, but not always, when I won I found that we had been playing for a penny. But although I did not see much of him, it soon became a comfort just to know that he was there, a kind of security against troubles becoming too serious, which they sometimes threatened to do. The person in whose despite I had sat in the pail was still his housekeeper. I don't think that she was to blame; I merely made larger demands on patience than she could satisfy. But the consequences were often distressing.

On Sundays, however, I saw much more of my Grandfather. Every other week I went to church with him in the morning, and on alternate Sundays for a walk. Church always bored me dreadfully, and made me melancholy. I think it was because it bored my Grandfather too that he would only go once a fortnight, which was a great relief to me, as he liked me for a companion on his walks. The rest of the family frowned, but though he was a very mild old man he was master in his own house. I remember only one morning service distinctly. After breakfast I had made a cigar of brown paper and attempted to smoke it. As I was going to church I felt unwell, and, as the service proceeded, worse. During the psalms I was sick over the chair of a lady sitting in front of me, and was ignominiously led out under the cold gaze of a disapproving congregation.

But the walks *were* walks. These, and my school games and my holidays were the almost adequate compensations for church, lessons, and the distempers of Winchester Road. There will be more to say of them. I became a pupil at the Oxford High School, whose name has since, no doubt for sufficient reasons, been changed to the City of Oxford School. It was something over a mile from home, and I used to walk there and back along St. Giles's twice a day, except half-holidays, unless the snow was heavy, when I took my dinner with me in a paper bag. I still have a scar on my shin to remind me of a fall in jumping the iron railings of the church at the fork of the Woodstock and Banbury Roads, when a boy named Bruton carried me home on his back. The only three landmarks on my journeys that I recall vividly were the Ratcliffe Observatory with its little balls on top, the Martyrs' Memorial, and a bun-shop in St. Giles's where the window was dressed in a way that I greatly admired.

I began in the First Form, and although in six years I rose to the Fifth, I did so without credit of any kind. I was awarded only two prizes in that time. One was a form prize, and was in the nature of a superannuation when I had outgrown the rest of the form by two or three terms; the other was for chemistry, and this I am sure must have been given me by mistake. For the rest, I took not the smallest interest in any of my classes from first to last. What gift my masters may have had for teaching I cannot say; I certainly displayed none for learning. And yet I liked my school, and although I cannot say that it awakened any intellectual life in me, I got a good deal out of it. It was chiefly through the games.

I had a natural taste and some aptitude for these, and here at all events we were lucky in our masters. B. O. Corbett has always remained for me the greatest outside left who ever kicked a football, and both he and his brother A. L. were on the staff. Both played for the Varsity, and B. O. got an international cap as well. They set in the school a soccer standard that in later years has produced such players as A. H. G. Kerry and A. H. Phillips, and under their example I learnt to adore the game. Those were the days of G. O. Smith, and to be playing centre-forward for the High School seemed somehow to link one's destiny with his. And besides the Corbetts there were G. Holloway and L. M. Phillips, the one thick-set and powerful, the other long and raking, both playing for the crack city amateurs, The Cygnets. Phillips had another claim on my attention. Each day at the morning interval he sent one of the boys from the playground to buy seven doughnuts for sixpence from a neighbouring baker. The wage for this errand was one doughnut, and I had a passion for doughnuts. I am under the impression that Phillips himself ate the remaining six, but he may have given one or two away.

Holloway was also our star performer at cricket, playing for Oxford County. He took a real interest in the school eleven, and used to encourage us with little personal kindnesses. One of my perquisites was his daily copy of *The Sportsman*, and once, when I was walking along the canal to some ground I saw him waiting for me with a pair of his old pads, which he gave to me. It was a very distinguished thing to have a pair of one's own. Once, when I was small, he caught me fouling an opponent at playground football, and talked to me in a way that I remember after thirty-five years. I can honestly say that I never fouled anyone again. Holloway was, in all senses, a stout fellow. He and Phillips were great friends, and they came to a tragic end together. They both received appointments to Bangkok in Siam, and went out on the same boat. On the evening of their arrival, Phillips was down with yellow fever. Holloway nursed him through the night, to see him die in the morning, and before the day was out he was dead himself of the same sickness.

# III

SOME other masters I remember. The Head was Mr. Cave, who in his honoured retirement will not mind my recalling the fact that to my generation he was known as Tubby. (Since these lines were written he has died.) I often wonder whether schoolmasters know these things. I hope so. He was a mathematician, a science in which I exhibited a minimum of talent, well beneath such august notice. But occasionally there were visits to his room of an alarming nature, though I must say that he always treated me with great forbearance. One encounter of another kind may be reserved for later telling. Then there was Jeffreys of the Second Form, who decided that my name was too long and shortened it to D'Ater, as which I thenceforth appeared on his school lists and was known till the end of my time. H. R. Hall, a parson with an aspect like the perennial youth of Apollo, kept the one boarding house, which I was later to join. He dispensed a gentle irony from the table of the Fourth, but I was less frightened of him, I think, than of anyone else on the staff. He brought good manners into the class-room.

Also he wrote a school song containing the arresting line:

*What a rock is H. G. Belcher.*

Belcher was, I suppose, the most remarkable man in the school, a genuine 'character.' His class methods were terrifying. He was a classic, with a considerable reputation as a private coach, and when I went up to him in the Fifth my Latin was deplorable. Daily, as he told me to translate a passage, I stood up in panic and made ridiculous guesses, spellbound into what I knew to be futility. And daily my exhibition would be cut short by a contemptuous roar, if not by an infuriated figure charging at me across the room with a gown flourished as in the wind. I was berated, and sometimes I was thwacked. It made no difference, and after a time he gave it up, contenting himself by making me write out any broken rule twenty times. As I broke twenty or so at a lesson or in a single prose, I was in daily attendance for the full imposition time from four till five in the afternoon.

Nevertheless, I had an affection for **H. G. B.** He knew it, and apart from his furies, was kind to me. When not excited by classic transgressions, he administered rebuke with an icy humour. Once, just as we had assembled in form from prayers in the hall, he addressed me:

'Oh, Drinkwater?'

(*rising*) 'Yes, sir.'

'I ask merely out of curiosity. I am interested in other people's religious experiences. Don't answer if you would rather not. What is your objection to the Lord's Prayer?'

'What, sir?'

'The Lord's Prayer. What precisely is your objection to it?'

'I don't think I've got any, sir.'

'Then why don't you say it?'

But out of school we got on well together. Then my ignorance no longer exasperated, but amused him; moreover, he knew I liked things that he liked, swimming and mushrooming and bird's-nesting and taking photographs. I think he was rather an unhappy man; disappointed, perhaps, that some temperamental twist had confined his learning to the second mastership of a High School. His fancy was taken by a boy who already knew something of the Water Eaton meadows and Bagley Wood. Also he liked an enthusiasm for games, which he shared with awkward insufficiency, although it is true that when I got my cricket colours he observed that it merely showed the poor standard of the school. He was tall and muscular, with a high bald forehead; a rock. He was able to kick a football only in a straight line with his run, and had to deploy himself in the field in order to get into position for his approach. To interfere with the ball while he did this was daring to the point of rashness; it was risking pursuit and effacement by juggernaut. I was active enough sometimes to escape in possession, hearing over my shoulder a thunder of feet and muttered imprecations—'beast' or 'little pig.' But to meet his onset was to ensure disaster; his path was as that of the tornado; no one ever better heeded than he the injunction to keep straight on. He was probably the worst footballer in the world.

He had a Canadian canoe, and in this I used to be taken on summer afternoon expeditions. I did the paddling, while he lay on his back among cushions, smoking Melachrino cigarettes. Tea was taken with us, and I boiled the water and washed the cups and plates afterwards. He used to make me swim from the bank to the canoe, increasing the distances until I became a tolerably good performer. I don't think we talked about anything in particular, but he was the first person I knew who seemed to find it worth while to drift about the backwaters and look among the reeds for a moorhen's nest, or tie up to a willow to watch the haymakers working with their broad wooden rakes. Apart from his classics he took not much interest in books, or if he did, told me nothing of it. Shortly before I left school he gave me my choice between a book and a Diamond Jubilee medal; I took the medal—which I still have—and he said it was very sensible of me.

I saw him once again some years after I left. I went down to Oxford from Birmingham for my Uncle Charles's funeral. I was to spend the evening with Belcher and return by the midnight train. I called on him at his Walton Street lodgings at eight o'clock, and had supper. At about half-past ten he announced that just now a desirable moth frequented the lamps of Woodstock Road. Providing me with an old bicycle, he set off on a new free-wheeler at a great pace, like a lancer, with a long cane-shafted butterfly net over his shoulder. He bade me follow, which I did laboriously in a black frock coat and a tweed cap that he lent me in place of my top hat. In any place but Oxford I must have excited curiosity in the police. My last recollection of him is a rather fine, aggressive face, turned up to the lamp-light, and ungraceful arms jerking the net for its prey. He died before he was old.

## IV

THE boys of thirty-five years ago come up again like ghosts, mostly little faded ghosts on old photographs. Sometimes in Oxford I see a name on a doorplate, and go in to find a lawyer or a wine-merchant, bald perhaps, or grey, out of whose face looks a remote urchin, on another who looks back at him. 'Bless me, you haven't changed,' is the formula. Curiously, it is true. The lines and the deepening contours, the scriptures and the almond-blossom, are strangely transparent disguises of a countenance known in youth. And it is the old image, not the new, or rather, the young, not the old, that attends these later meetings. As we talk, the untried features of twelve define themselves intensely, serenely, behind the mask of forty-seven.

Strange, too, is the insistency without such renewals. Returning lately to the school, I looked over an old album of the early 'nineties. There I found myself in a little straw hat with a bulging crown, standing at the end of the back row among the members of the Lower Third. Ghost by ghost they spoke their names, no one of them hesitating—Salter, Hurcomb, Webb, Zacharias, Wintle, Kent, Gardiner, and the rest. I had seen but one or two of them since the days when the discoloured silver print was made —a chance moment with Salter, who is, I believe, now the League of Nations, and a lunch or two with Hurcomb, who is the Ministry of Transport. No; the recollections had lain those five-and-thirty years in hiding, tacit and unsuspected, to spring up, fresh and supple, at the summons of an old photograph.

Three times at school I suffered serious indignity. Galpin, now City Coroner of Oxford—I wonder if he can remember. My weekly pocket-money allowance was threepence. But the Disciplinarian of Winchester Road made threepence a matter of intricate finance. The sum was represented by twelve cardboard discs—four for each penny. For every misdemeanour, according to its gravity, a fine was fixed; as, one disc for untidiness, two for being late, three for disobedience. In consequence, Saturday morning usually found a debit balance against me; a penny credit was phenomenal. Casual, and undisclosed, profits from cribbage were commonly all that stood between myself and destitution. After one prolonged period of economic reverses, my fortitude deserted me. Galpin and I sat next each other in the Second, and one morning I begged a penny of him. He was very displeased, and resisted for a long time, but at length I begged it. I spent it on the way home at dinner time, and then became exceedingly uncomfortable about it. In the afternoon I tried to avoid Galpin, which was difficult, sitting next to him. In the way of the world, I conceived an uneasy dislike towards him for being able to give me a penny. The next morning he told me that his father wished to see me, and I was terrified. I was sure that somehow I had not begged but stolen the penny. I refused to go, but he said I must. His father, also, was Coroner; I had a notion that he was the principal policeman. After much persuasion I went, almost sick with fear as I climbed the stairs of his office. I was, he understood, a friend of his son. I was. He liked to see his son's friends. 'Yes, sir,' very faintly, with dry lips, hating him for delaying the blow. Would I, perhaps, come to tea on Saturday? I would ask if I might. Yes, that would be very nice, dismissing me. And then, as I went bewildered to the door, 'Oh, by the way, put this in your pocket'—a half-crown. Not a word of the penny. As I walked home, I made a revaluation of life. I told nobody about it. But if ever half a crown bought a man's title to heaven, Mr. Galpin is there.

My other embarrassments had no such auspicious relief. I was supposed to look after my own clothes; I didn't. One wet morning as I was leaving for

school, it was found that my boot-soles needed
mending. I ought, it seems, to have known this
and done something about it. I had no others for
bad weather, and in spite of all protests Disciplinarian made me go to school in a pair of her own.
I suppose there was no alternative, but the humilia-
tion was dreadful. They were the old high-buttoned
kind that women used to wear, with scallop-shaped
tops that reached nearly to my knees. I slunk along
St. Giles's, and waited outside the playground until
the bell rang. I spent the morning in agonised and
futile efforts to hide my legs. How I got home I do
not know. The weather had cleared by dinner-time,
and I was allowed to go back humanly shod in the
afternoon.

Though this was a bad business, there was a
worse. We had no official tuck-shop, but the school
patronised the baker of the doughnuts, famous also
for fatty-cakes. By the doorway of the shop was a
large sack of broken biscuits, sold at a clearance
price. It was a recognised if furtive practice for boys
who had made other purchases to help themselves to
a pinch of these scraps on leaving. One day as I did
this, the shopman accosted me. 'Come here.' I went
to the counter. 'What have you got in your pocket?'
I produced them: 'Biscuits.' 'Where did you get
them from?' He had seen me take them, and I knew

it, but I lost my head. 'From home.' 'Oh, I see. You come from Mr. Brown's in Cornmarket, don't you?' 'Yes.' 'All right.' I heard no more of it, but although I was at the school three years longer, until I was fifteen, I never went into the shop again.

## V

My refuge, in these and all other anxieties, was my Grandfather. I did not tell him actually of particular troubles, but to be with him was soothing. Also, he liked doing the things that I liked, and he talked to me about serious matters, sometimes in a way that I did not understand, but always in a way that interested me.

His household consisted of my Uncle Charles, Disciplinarian, my sister and myself, and the servants. My sister soon went to a convent school in Belgium, and afterwards became a nun. Between Uncle Charles and myself an entirely undemonstrative friendship grew up, founded largely on a common hostility towards Disciplinarian. Once or twice he took me fishing for roach and perch at Thrupp, and one spring night he came up to my bedroom and waked me to show me some thrush's eggs in a box of primroses that he had brought back from the country. After a time he found Winchester Road tiresome, and took rooms in a farm-house out at Cumnor, where he was near to the lady to whom he was engaged. I called there once in his absence, with a schoolfellow, announced that I was Mr. Brown's nephew, and suggested that we should be fed. The farmer's wife placed a new ham before us, and left me to carve it. I have never been able to carve well, and Uncle Charles sent a somewhat heated message to Winchester Road. But on the whole he put up with me indulgently, and I liked him. I was glad when after long waiting he was able to marry the lady, who was always very agreeable to me. She had a nephew who was a great swell at bird's-nesting, and once when I was in funds I bought an owl's egg from him for twopence.

Of the servants I can remember only two, dimly. There was my Grandfather's man, who had a bald head and rather a hot temper. One day he threw a two-foot rule at me, but shortly afterwards when I was knocking walnuts off the tree in the garden I had the satisfaction of dislodging a piece of dead wood which bounced off his baldness. Then there was Elizabeth, the cook-general, who made remarkable soda-cakes and had leanings towards the Band of Hope. Sometimes I was taken by her to this organisation's pleasant Sunday afternoons, and I remember still some verses of a fighting temperance anthem that we used to sing. My Drinkwater ancestors, coaching-publicans of whom I have to tell,

would have listened with astonishment to a sprig
of their name singing in a shrill and tuneless treble:

> No matter what landlords say,
> We're going to clear the way!
> Our army's rising
> All surprising,
> Deeds of bravery
> Banish slavery,
> All get ready for the strife,
> We're going to clear the way!

But Winchester Road for me meant my Grandfather. The Sunday morning walks were seldom out
of Oxford, and usually took us to call on some
friend. The most interesting of these was Mr. Boswell, who had a face like one of the Apostles on the
Sheldonian Theatre. His business was trunk-making
in the Cornmarket, but he was also a celebrated authority on mosses, and he used to give me lessons
with an enchanted microscope. Under his guidance
I started a collection of my own, and I still know
*tortula muralis* when I see it. His room always had
a strong peaty smell, which I found very grateful.
I understood that he had important correspondence
about mosses from all parts of the world, and when
he died I believe his collection went to Kew
Gardens. Another point of call was at a rich uncle's,
where my Grandfather took sherry and biscuits, and

I a piece of seed-cake. This uncle's first wife had been my Mother's sister, one of the belles of Oxford. He drove a carriage, and seemed to me grander, I am sure, than he meant to be. His name was Sydenham Rowell, and I somehow associated him with the Crystal Palace.

As we walked, my Grandfather talked to me freely and easily. It is strange that I can recall clearly everything about him but the tones of his voice—I think that perhaps nothing fades so easily from an intimate memory. He was deliberate in all his movements; it would take him several minutes to fill his pipe and light it with a fusee, the end of which he used to leave sticking out of the bowl as he smoked. He liked best talking about history and sport, and occasionally politics. He said that there was only one thing that he had ever hated in the world, and that was Mr. Gladstone. He thought the greatest Englishman was the Duke of Wellington, and Walter Scott the greatest poet.

In the summer he was fond of watching the University play cricket in the Parks, and when I was free on a half-holiday I used to go with him and sit on the grass beside his camp stool. Those were the Oxford days of Fry and the Palairets, but there were two players who came to no such fame, and yet were remarkable in their promise as undergraduates.

One was G. J.—I think those were the initials—
Mordaunt, who had a style not excelled by L. C. H.
Palairet himself, and the other was F. H. E. Cunliffe, who seems to me to have hit the stumps more
often than any other slow bowler I ever saw. I remember him with peculiar clearness because one
Sunday morning, as my Grandfather and I were
walking along Bevington Road, we saw Cunliffe's
round-shouldered figure approaching. My Grandfather said he would speak to him. I didn't see how
he could without being introduced, but as we met
the thing happened. 'Excuse me, sir,' said seventy
very ceremoniously to twenty-two, 'but I should like
to tell you how very much I admire your bowling.'
As my Grandfather now appeared to know Mr. Cunliffe, it seemed to me that I might myself hope for
an introduction, but somehow that was not ordained,
and I stood respectfully on the curb as the hero of
a hundred wickets replied, 'That's very good of you,
sir,' and departed, while I called attention to myself
by raising my cap.

On week-days I had my meals in a school-room. I
remember nothing of it but a horse-hair sofa, in the
grain of which my own hair used sometimes painfully to get caught when I lay upon it. It was here
that one day Disciplinarian found me reading a
penny-dreadful, my earliest taste in literature. Not

exactly found me, since I heard her approaching, and hid the paper-covered book by thrusting it up under the elastic-drawn knee of my knickerbockers. She was of a suspicious nature, however, and my fault was detected. I was told that to read such things was not merely wrong, but wicked. If she were a man I should certainly and deservedly be beaten; as it was, I should be fined twelve discs this week, and twelve next. I think her judgment, which resulted in my introduction to the more refined romances of G. A. Henty, was right.

But on Sundays the family took midday dinner with my Grandfather in the dining-room. It was rather a solemn room, with its mahogany bookcase containing several sets of bound magazines, and a table-window displaying a large-leaved ficus-plant. I sat facing two prints on the wall which much took my fancy—'The Attack' and 'The Defeat,' representing a boy before and after the assault on an entire apple-pie. The dinner was always a very good one, particularly when there was crackling on the pork, but for its very finest relish there had to be an announcement from my Grandfather that we were to walk out into the country for tea. For these were the real walks, taken every other week or so from early spring until late autumn. They were journeys to my Broceliande.

# VI

BROCELIANDE was, in fact, four or five Oxfordshire farms, owned by various members of the Brown family. These places furnished my mind with intimacies that could never fade. These many years later, there are still sights and sounds that renew emotions then first experienced, fugitive yet exquisitely sharp and vivid in their flight, poignant with a physical intensity, and yet intangible, eluding expression, realised only by some sixth sense. I learnt in those days a good deal about the practical life of the farms, and if put to it I could still drive a plough or build a sheepfold or load a wagon. But it is of subtler, remoter detail that I speak. When I see garden-violets growing in the shelter of a brick wall, or smell buttermilk, or hear a yellowhammer calling a-little-bit-of-bread-and-no-cheese from a hedge, I do not merely recall these things as known in childhood, but am aware of a veil almost lifted upon I know not what mystery that yet has in it the assurance of an old and simple familiarity.

I spent nearly all my holidays on these farms, that is to say three months of each year. But the two that we could reach on our Sunday afternoon walks were at Elsfield and Wood Eaton. Once out into the fields, the path to the Elsfield farm was all enchantment. First there was the ferry to be crossed, with its bell and the wire rope worn smooth by the hands of the ferryman. Then the hill road with its high green banks up into the village, and at the end of it a laconic grunt of welcome from Cousin John, with his friendly weathered face and boots soled an inch thick. The stone floor of the hall and the side-table that was ornamented always with an incredible quantity of driving gloves are still evocations of that queer, impalpable kind, and still more so is the little conservatory opening from the parlour, about which many years later I wrote a poem called 'History':

Sometimes, when walls and occupation seem
A prison merely, a dark barrier
Between me everywhere
And life, or the larger province of the mind,
As dreams confined,
As the trouble of a dream,
I seek to make again a life long gone,
To be
My mind's approach and consolation,
To give it form's lucidity,
Resilient form, as porcelain pieces thrown
In buried China by a wrist unknown,
Or mirrored brigs upon Fowey sea.

Then to my memory comes nothing great
Of purpose, or debate,
Pomp, nor love's rapture, nor heroic hours to
  spend,
But most, and strangely, for long and so much have
  I seen,
Comes back an afternoon
Of a June
Sunday at Elsfield, that is up on a green
Hill, and there,
Through a little farm parlour door,
A floor
Of red tiles and blue,
And the air
Sweet with the hot June sun cascading through
The vine-leaves under the glass, and a scarlet fume
Of geranium flower, and soft and yellow bloom
Of musk, and stains of scarlet and yellow glass.

Such are the things remain
Quietly, and for ever, in the brain,
And the things that they choose for history-making
  pass.

There was always an egg for tea at Elsfield, or,
if one liked, two. Also there was much to be discovered about cowsheds, rickyards, and orchards. My
cousin John's conversation was of an exceedingly
lugubrious character, as became a member of a
farming family.

# INHERITANCE

Let the wealthy and great
Roll in splendour and state
I envy them not I declare it;
I eat my own lamb,
My own chickens and ham,
I shear my own fleece and I wear it;

I have lawns, I have bowers,
I have fruits, I have flowers,
The lark is my morning alarmer,
So jolly boys now
Here's God speed the plough,
Long life and success to the Farmer.

How benignly the verses ring on their Staffordshire
pots, so gaily decorated with an inventory of implements, ploughs and scythes, forks and rakes, hedg-
ing-bills and gauntlets, Giles lifting his glass pros-
perously to his wife as she works at her hand-churn.
The festoons and sheaves of plenty accord prettily
enough with the sentiment; but this, I fear, is the
kind of poetry that Rosalind declared to be feign-
ing. For the reflection here given of the farmer's
mind is, in my experience, an inaccurate one. The
Browns of Oxfordshire were a thriving lot. They
lived like fighting-cocks, shot and hunted two days
a week, brought up large families, cut figures at
point-to-point and the agricultural shows, and if the
truth were known I have no doubt that they could

show tight little balances at the bank. And yet to hear them talk one would suppose that the advent of the bailiffs could with difficulty be delayed another fortnight at most. For John, indeed, a fortnight was usually too sanguine an estimate. It seemed, rather, that next Sunday would hardly find him still master of his own farm. He was, in fact, quite substantial, and as happy as most men, but he cherished the coming dissolution of his fortune as a saint his repentance. His complaint was full of resource. The weather was the durnedest that had ever plagued mortal man, hay wouldn't pay for carting, beasts were doing no good on cake at six pounds a ton, wages—eleven shillings a week—were out of all sense, manure was up, mutton down, and in general the fly was very extensively on the turnip. As he spoke, his face glowed with dejection. Should he pitch the feeling but one note higher, it seemed that he must break into operatic sobs.

Elsfield has a further particular memory for me. The village cricket was run by another farmer, and, long before I was in my school eleven, I challenged his team to a bank-holiday match. He must have thought that rather uppish of me, but he took it in good part and accepted. I then had to face the somewhat delicate problem of getting a worthy side together. It was to be a day match, and Elsfield undertook to provide lunch and tea in a tent, which was a good beginning. I then put the case before my Uncle Charles, and he promised to stand a two-horse brake to and from Elsfield. Armed with these inducements, I approached the school cricket captain —it was Andrews I;—and asked for his co-operation. At first he was doubtful as to the propriety of encouraging the irregular activities of small boys, but the attractions overweighed his scruples. Then things took an awkward turn. He said that he would treat it as a school match, which meant that he would select the team, and that I had no reasonable chance of being included in it. He said that he would put the eleven up on the board in a day or two. I thanked him and falsely said how pleased I was. Four days of bitter—I think it really was bitter—anxiety went by and nothing happened, while I reflected that somehow I had bungled my opportunity. Then the list appeared, and on it to my inexpressible relief I read the name of Drinkwater as eleventh man.

The excursion was a complete success. I can't remember who won, but Elsfield turned out in force to cheer the exploits of an alarming fast bowler who was known as The Plunger. The weather was fine, there was a lavish supply of sausage rolls and jam tarts, with ginger beer and even some without ginger, and Uncle Charles wore flannel trousers. I had enough sense to keep myself discreetly in the background, and on the return journey was rewarded by a deliberate expression of thanks from Andrews on behalf of the school for what he was pleased to call a jolly good day.

# VII

THE other Sunday afternoon farm was at Wood Eaton, rather a longer walk than Elsfield from Oxford. Here the farmer was Tom Brown, the best horseman and the best shot in the family. He was little and whipcordy, with a face like a smiling Ribston pippin. He was justly esteemed for insight and good sense, and no member of the Brown clan, for they were a clannish lot, ever failed to turn to him in a difficulty. Here is a tree of the clan as I remember it, incomplete, and, no doubt, containing errors in the matter of seniority.

They carried family solidarity to unusual lengths, Arthur, Charles, and Albert, the sons of Thomas, marrying respectively Mary, Annie, and Avis, the daughters of William, with prolific and, it may be added, robust consequences.

Tom of Wood Eaton had a romantic interest for me as the hero of a legendary scene in the Piddington orchard. Like most of his brothers and cousins he was in the Yeomanry, and as a younger man he was on one occasion about to leave his father's house for the annual training. Parents and sisters and

# THE THREE BROTHERS

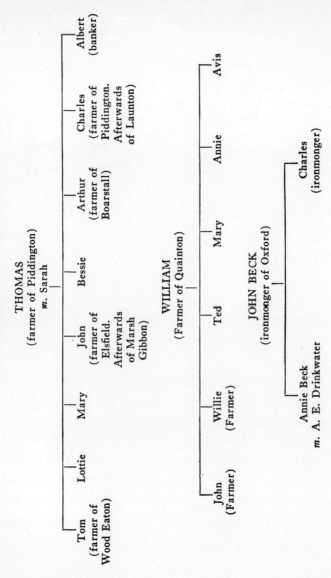

THOMAS
(farmer of Piddington)
*m.* Sarah

Tom (farmer of Wood Eaton) — Lottie — Mary — John (farmer of Elsfield. Afterwards of Marsh Gibbon) — Bessie — Arthur (farmer of Boarstall) — Charles (farmer of Piddington. Afterwards of Launton) — Albert (banker)

WILLIAM
(Farmer of Quainton)

John (Farmer) — Willie (Farmer) — Ted — Mary — Annie — Avis

JOHN BECK
(ironmonger of Oxford)

Annie Beck
*m.* A. E. Drinkwater — Charles (ironmonger)

farm-hands were assembled to witness the departure, when in full uniform, frogs and sword and busby, he mounted a young horse, which promptly took fright, bolted down the orchard, and threw its rider. To the horror of the spectators, a cavalry boot stuck in the stirrup, and Tom was dragged by the terrified animal in a zigzag course among the apple-trees, Aunt Sarah's screams intensifying the panic as the men folk strove to stop disaster short of the worst. Tradition had it that several minutes passed before the runaway, with its unfortunate victim, was brought to a standstill. But Tom Brown was not dead. He got on to his feet, went indoors and brushed himself, and in less than five minutes rode off to camp without changing his mount. When I knew him, he looked that sort of man, and I don't believe that there was a better or a kinder in Oxfordshire.

I stayed but once or twice at Quainton. My Great-uncle William had died before I first went; the red farm house fronting across the village green, and overtopped by the great sails of a windmill, was in the joint tenancy of his three sons, a string of as fine athletic-looking fellows as you could meet. A peculiarly satisfactory feature of the household was the presence of a large fruit pie each morning on the breakfast table, with a pint jug of cream. On the sideboard also was a larger jug of beer, in which as yet I took no interest. It was here that I first fell in love, with my Cousin Avis, then, I suppose, about twenty. When I went away she gave me a nickel-plated pig, which was a match-box. I still have it, though the plate has long since worn down to its primal brass.

Miss Doris Arthur Jones in the life of her father, Henry Arthur, speaks of his people as coming from March Gibbon. I wonder what authority there is for March. Marsh Gibbon it always was to me. John Brown went from Elsfield to farm there while I was still at school, and although I visited it but seldom the place is associated in my mind with one Homeric day. In the winter holidays I missed no opportunity of running with the Bicester hounds. Two or three of the Brown brothers were notable performers with the pack, and once at breakfast I remember Charles and Arthur receiving from Lord Valentia, the Master, sets of cuff-links made of gold-mounted fox-teeth. It was esteemed an event of much distinction in the family.

On the day in question, the meet was in the Marsh Gibbon country, and I was there. By many devious ways we later found ourselves in the Earl of Jersey's park at Middleton Stoney, and there in the laurel gardens I saw a fox suddenly double on his tracks when the nearest hound was within striking distance, drive clean through the pack in full cry, and get away. The initiated may condemn it for an improbable fiction, but there it was. As improbable, perhaps, as another incident, this one ornithological. I once found a thrush's nest in the paddock at Piddington. Before it was ready for laying, a thunderstorm washed away the still wet mud of its little circular wall. A week or so later it had been appropriated by another tenant, and contained a clutch of blackbird's eggs.

From Middleton Stoney hounds went home, and in the early dusk I started off on the seven miles back to Marsh Gibbon. At the end of them I had run and walked over twenty-five in the day, and I rewarded myself by eating four boiled eggs for tea.

It was Anthony Hine who said that fox-hunting was parlous. I was not sure what he meant, but his tone was not complimentary. Anthony, however, was not very right in his wits, and his opinions had little credit in the countryside which he used to walk for casual jobs, cleaning out a yard or chopping wood. In the latter process he once sent a stout beech-stick spinning on to my cheek-bone, which still bears the mark. That established friendly relations between us, but the plummy thickness of his speech made conversation difficult. He was a figure fantastic almost to the point of grandeur. He must have been six foot six inches tall, was inconceivably thin, and with arms of inordinate length and a fringe of grizzled beard and whisker, he resembled a greatly elongated scarecrow. He wore a tattered tail-coat, trousers with frayed edges that reached only to his bare calves, derelict boots, and a jaunty pork-pie cap. He walked very fast with immense strides and a limp, and he had a squint that seemed to be not of two but three dimensions. He was commonly reported to be harmlessly mad. Harmless he certainly was, but as for the madness, I suspect that there were several hawks that he knew from herneshaws. To the general astonishment it was one day announced that Anthony was going to be married. This meant sport for the countryside, but a wily vicar stole a march on conspiracy by wedding the remarkable couple at six o'clock in the morning. I say couple, for though I never saw Anthony's partner in this alarming romance, remarkable she must have been.

# VIII

School holidays were the fulfilment of those Sunday afternoon glimpses of a promised land, for then I came into possession for weeks on end. The central point in the country that I knew so familiarly was Piddington, a village four miles south-east of Bicester. Marsh Gibbon is three and a half miles to the north, and Boarstall two to the south. These were the places, Piddington and Boarstall, that were mapped in my mind, cottage by cottage and field by field. Bicester was the nearest station to Piddington, the line not then passing, as it now does, through Ludgershall a mile to the east. There are still old men in England who have never travelled beyond their own valley or wood-side, to whom the landscape three miles away is 'foreign country.' So it was with myself in boyhood. I knew what kind of moss grew on which walls in Piddington, and would miss a bramble creeper that a year before had been trailing on the water of a ditch. A repaired gate, a rearrangement of the glass jars of bull's-eyes and acid drops in the tiny shop window, the cutting of a haystack, the removal of a horseshoe from the forge wall, the change of cattle from one pasture to another—these things were inevitably noted. But of places off my usual rounds I knew nothing.

> Brill on the hill,
> Oakley in the hole,
> Shabby little Ickford
> And dirty Worminghall—

I could have come to any of them in an hour's walk, and I never saw one. For all times of day, all weathers, and all seasons, there was enough and to spare of interest, even of excitement, in the few lanes and acres that I knew as well as I knew the contents of my own pockets. Far wandering had no attractions for me. I would always rather go to see a nest in the home close four times a day than find a new one in the next parish.

The influence of landscape on character is deep and incalculable. Natural grandeur would seem to be inadequately reflected in the people born to it. Switzerland and the Arizonas are not remarkable as sources of inspiration. Burns came not from the Grampians, but from the uneventful lowlands of Ayrshire. Wordsworth lived among the noblest scenery in England, and loved it, but his poetic life was largely an effort to subdue the majesty of Helvellyn to the intimacies of a cottage and its garden.

Where in England are the painters who have been taught by spectacular nature as were a few quiet men by their Suffolk and Norfolk levels?

Perhaps the more dramatic manifestations of earth discourage rather than invite emulation. Certain it is that vision and invention have attended more closely upon her reticences. The Dutch and Flemish masters found revelation in her domestic moods, and the English muse has never been happier than in Warwickshire or the Thames water-meadows. It is not a question of beauty; a hedgerow in primrose time or a spinney of larch-buds can match the Alps or the Golden Gate in beauty. It is a question of scale and composition. The vaster and the more elaborate these become, the less, it would seem, is the soil of imagination fertilised. The sublimer convulsions of nature make us marvel, they do not make us prophesy. The poets of the eighteenth century who found the heights of Hampstead or the Sussex downs terrifying were not so wide of the mark as might be supposed. Even the Mediterranean peoples, the Spaniards, the Italians and the Greeks, have enriched the world with loveliness drawn not from their wilder landscape, but from tranquil vineyards and hill-sides and market-places—a tranquillity transfigured, it is true, in its especial splendour of sun and blue skies and waters.

Athens, it must be remembered, was not fabulously renowned to Æschylus. Travel, which takes us delightfully to the things and places so properly advertised as worth seeing, may enlarge conversation, it may even broaden the mind, but I doubt whether it has much or any effect on character. It may produce good travel books; it seldom produces poetry. The character and the poetry in us are fostered by contacts more casual, and more abiding. We arrange to see the Pyramids or Teneriffe, but we do not arrange to be born on a Yorkshire moor or in a Dorset village. And the less the moor or the village may seem to assert itself, the more profoundly will it possess us, instruct us, become memorable.

No traveller has ever gone a yard out of his way to visit Piddington; none ever will. A farmer walking a fox-hound puppy down the street is an event there, and there is nothing to earn even the dust of a star from Baedeker. It is a plain, grey little village, neutral in design, ambling from cottage to cottage with no apparent sense of direction, its half dozen larger houses of red brick sitting discreetly here and there at the roadside as if they were nobody in particular. It lies at the foot of a trifling hill, in a flat acreage too modest to be called a plain. When I knew it, a stranger was seen only when one passed through in the carrier's cart, or when the Irish labourers came over for hay-harvest, a talkative, thirsty lot, sleeping in the lofts and barns. In the winter, when icicles were on the thatch-eaves, the village would lie for days as if it were asleep.

Nevertheless, life there, by its very economy of effect, was vivid. Everything that happened had its roots in custom, old necessity, fitness. Not once in a year, or five, was that gentle but robust sufficiency startled. I remember seeing a strange dog-cart outside the cottage of a farm-labourer who was a friend of mine. A sympathetic little group of onlookers told me that it belonged to the Bicester police, who had come to take my friend away. I saw him brought out of his cottage and driven off. The offence, I believe, was not a serious one, but the sensation hung over the countryside for months. Piddington was as old as that. So engendering was its frugal reality that after thirty years and more I can still remember the shape of the rookery trees, the plodding of the horse round the churn track, the taste of the little summer apples, one side rosy, and the other true apple-green, in the orchard. I can remember, too, the wasps in the William pears.

# IX

WHEN I first knew it, the Piddington farm was in the holding of my Great-uncle Thomas, my Grandfather's elder brother, and father of the many sons and daughters aforesaid. Of these, all but Charles and Bessie had left home to be married. The household was completed by its mistress, my Great-aunt Sarah.

The effect of the industrial revolution on rural life during the closing quarter of the eighteenth century can hardly have been greater than that of mechanical development during the first of the twentieth. The Piddington farm as I knew it in the early 'nineties was effectively a patriarchal establishment. Its daily life, remote from a station, was scarcely influenced by the railways, and the roads knew nothing faster than horse-traffic. The isolation made of the family and the farm-workers a self-dependent organism, of which for weeks at a time no member would go further afield than to Bicester market. There was but one post a day, and no telephone. A couple of concerts, parochial concerts, in the winter, a cricket match at Whitsuntide and another on

August Bank Holiday, a beanfeast at harvest-home and a blow-out at Christmas—these were the celebrated occasions for which the wage-earners waited, with long stretches of steady seasonal work between whiles. And then there were the public-houses, of which, as Mr. Shaw's Tarlton would say, read Chesterton. It was all a sadly insufficient life, doubtless, impoverished, without ambitions, and very apt for the operations of progress. They have better wages now, they know one of the world's best comedians as Charlie, and already they no longer trouble to look up from their fields when an aeroplane passes overhead.

Nevertheless, the bad old days had their points. The masters enjoyed the further diversions of hunting and shooting, and even, once in a while, of a day in Oxford, if not in London itself. But the norm of life was a settled and segregated feudalism, with good-will, security, and a steady babbling of green fields. The labour was exacting, but the pace was slow, the discipline easy. The apex of the day was dinner at noon in the large stone-flagged kitchen, cool in summer, warm and bright with roaring logs in winter. Here at one table assembled the family, with Uncle Thomas at its head, and augmented perhaps by the people from Boarstall or Marsh Gibbon or Wood Eaton, or by a small boy from school.

Along the wall at the other end of the room were a bench and long board laid for such of the farm-hands as chose to come in. The fare was feudal too, for its plenty was almost entirely of home production. They baked their own bread, churned their own butter, pressed their own cheese, brewed their own beer, killed and cured their own bacon, grew their own fruit and vegetables, took their own corn to a local mill for flour, brought in their own eggs, found their own game and poultry, and on occasion whetted their appetites with their own cowslip wine. The only important purchase that had to be made was meat, and consequently there was some economy in its use. This was effected in one way that was particularly pleasing to me. When a joint was to be served, it was preceded always by a leviathan of apple puddings, upon which the first zest of hunger was to spend itself. In my own case, certainly, the stratagem was unfailing, since for me apple pudding was, and has always remained, desirable beyond the primest cut of any. Sometimes instead of pudding it was dumplings, which are co-equal in rank. In either case, by the time I had finished my lavish allowance, I was well content with what the eating-houses used to call a follow of roast.

During my holidays at Piddington and Boarstall, I worked quite seriously for my living, taking on regular duties according to the season of the year. Before breakfast and at tea-time I brought the cows up from the fields for milking, learning the precise intonations for 'Coop-coop-coop-coop-come-along-come-along.' Twice a day I went round the hen-houses with a basket for eggs, and sometimes had the satisfaction of finding a straggler's nest in the undergrowth of an outlying hedge. I led plough, turned hay, gleaned stubble, topped swedes, and fed the threshing-machine from the rick. The last named occupation was attended by the final excitement of turning up incredible quantities of mice as the last fan-like sheaves were lifted by the fork from the ground. I remember my sinister delight when a visitor, who I thought was overdressed, ran round the rick-yard in a panic, a mouse having run up the inside of his trouser-leg.

A more serious catastrophe really frightened me. The bee-master at Boarstall was about to take a swarm, wearing his gauntlets and gauze helmet, when a stranger walked towards the hives to watch. He was warned away, and was in the act of explaining that nobody could teach him anything about bees, when the swarm broke up and buzzed in a cloud of fury round his head. He was eventually carried into my cousin's house, hideously stung, and it was several hours before he was able to leave, much disfigured, and wiser about bees than he had supposed was possible. It was at Boarstall too that I myself learnt something about wasps. On the way to a field with some village boys to play cricket, we passed a dung-hill which contained a nest. A boy a few yards in front of me shoved a stump into the hole, to which I came as the indignant occupants emerged. It is true that only four attached themselves to me, but I danced before the Lord, to be relieved only by liberal applications of the blue-bag.

Best of all, perhaps, were the late summer days when I went shepherding, with the dignity of having the job to myself. After breakfast, I went up into one of the larger fields, where the flock had been folded for the night. I had to let the sheep out, take down the stakes and hurdles and place them in orderly piles, and then until evening keep my charges to a prescribed part of the field and away from forbidden crops. I took my dinner with me in a large handkerchief, usually bread and cheese, with a jam turnover, and, on lucky days, a peach or two. My holiday clothes never amounted to anything much, and after a week or so in the country I became a considerable ragamuffin. One day when I was minding sheep near a road with a gate across it, I saw a bicyclist approaching. On going to open the gate for him, I was disconcerted to find that it was

my headmaster, Mr. Cave. I said something about
sheep; he replied affably, and went on. I argued that
in the circumstances a somewhat disreputable appearance could hardly be accounted a breach of
school rules, but I had an uneasy feeling that I could
have explained better if Mr. Cave had given me more
time. However, I reassured myself that Tubby was
a good sort, and, indeed, misgivings could hardly
have had a slighter occasion. But fend alone and
knock about though I did, finding pleasure freely, I
was a needlessly anxious sort of child, fearful of
things that might go bump at any time of the day
or night. There was to be something of a fight in
later years to defeat these humours, and to declare
myself ineligible for the melancholy epitaph:

HERE LIES
JOHN JONES
WHOSE LIFE WAS FULL
OF TROUBLES
NONE OF WHICH
EVER HAPPENED

I can't say that on my long shepherding days I did
any hard thinking, or even that I was consciously
observant of nature. But it seems to me that I was
intensely aware of the life about me. Doing nothing
in particular beyond keeping an eye on the sheep, I

was neither lazy nor bored. Some energy that I did not realise was, I am sure, keeping my mind occupied, the growth and change of things, the ways of creatures, the movement of trees and hedgerows, the aspects of weather, the course of the sun and its shadows. I did not know what I was learning, or even that I was learning anything at all, but the instruction was to serve for a lifetime.

In late afternoon a boy would come down from the farm to help me put up the hurdles again, the stake-driving being too much for me single-handed. A new plot chosen, the fold set, and the sheep safely closed in, I would get home in time for high tea, and then cricket in the evening with the five or so aside, all fielding, that I was able to collect from the village.

# X

ONE of the principal events of the year at Piddington was the rook-shooting. The clump of high rookery elms stood but a few yards away from the house,
so that as one lay abed in the morning it sounded
as though the rooks were chattering somewhere up
above the roof. During the day the colony went
far off to its feeding-grounds, but at dusk the grave
chorus would be heard coming across the fields, and
the air was fussy with contented argument as the
Piddington rooks settled into the tree-tops for the
night.

With nesting time, however, there was more to be
attended to at home by day, and then the gossip was
unceasing. By the third week in May the young birds
were out on the boughs, fully fledged and effecting
short, clumsy flights. On the appointed day, soon
after breakfast the gigs began to arrive, bringing
perhaps eight guns, and a few visitors besides who
came to watch. Among them would be my Grandfather, who did not shoot, and my Uncle Charles,
who, on this occasion only, did.

Ethically, I suppose that all destructive sports

are indefensible, and yet I have little logic in the matter. I have always disliked shooting, and yet I go fishing whenever opportunity offers. When I was very young I was stupidly placed on a half-broken hunter which bolted with me, and I never took to riding afterwards, but to drift about after the hounds on foot has always been a delight to me. While, however, I enjoy the whole spectacle and scene and incident of fox-hunting, a spent fox inspires no enthusiasm in me whatever. I dare say it is all very weak-minded and inconsistent, but there it is. Blood-sports are cruel; they have, nevertheless, for centuries been the occasion of much that is most picturesque, sociable, and high-spirited in English life. When character plays these queer tricks with us, I do not know that it is any the less character.

I am afraid that it is a question upon which my own logic really goes to pieces altogether, and that I find myself making what are doubtless quite untenable distinctions. There may be no valid reason for distinguishing between a hooked trout and a stag at bay or a fox being dug out of its earth. But I indulge the sentimentality. And somehow, the shooting of young rooks as they sat confidently on their branches never seemed to me to be quite good enough. A flying partridge, for example, had a fair chance of being missed, but the young rook merely sat there until he got hit. At the same time, the ceremony of rook-shooting was one never to be forgotten.

The morning stand done, came lunch, cold, of which I can remember only tins of ginger-nuts and cracknels, and a very handsome cask of beer. On one occasion a young bailiff from a neighbouring farm was being much congratulated on some recent athletic exploit, and Uncle Charles took it into his head to lay that with a fair start I could beat him to the end of the paddock and back. The dispute was hotly taken up by the table. Immediately after lunch a handicap was fixed, betting became brisk, and the race took place. My rival, I suspect, had done too well by the sirloin and home-brew, for not only was he beaten, but he went a most disagreeable colour at the end of the race, and took an hour to recover.

As the afternoon wore on and the heap of dead rooks grew in size, there was each year a heated dispute between Uncle Thomas and Aunt Sarah as to their disposal. Those who knew the technique of the household, myself among them, waited for it attentively. There is in *She Stoops to Conquer* an obscure reference to which the commentators, I believe, have discovered no clue. 'Diggory,' says Mr. Hardcastle, 'you are too talkative. Then if I happen to say a good thing, or tell a good story at table, you must not all burst out a-laughing, as if you made part of the company.' To which Diggory retorts, 'Then ecod your worship must not tell the story of Ould Grouse in the gun-room: I can't help laughing at that for the soul of me. We have laughed at that these twenty years.'

When I first read that, I had an idea that if the secret were disclosed, it would turn out to have something to do with my Uncle Thomas and Aunt Sarah at rook-shooting. It generally began about four in the afternoon, when Aunt Sarah would say, innocently, 'Well, Thomas, we'll have the birds put in the coach-house.' 'Ay,' would come the answer. 'Or better put 'em in the gun-room.' And then the battle joined, family and guests finding discreet points of vantage as the antagonists went to it up and down the garden path that ran alongside the places in dispute.

*S.* I think the coach-house, Thomas.

*T.* Coach-house is no place for rooks. What's gun-room for?

*S.* I won't have rooks inside the house. Crawling like they do. You ought to have more sense.

*T.* I tell 'ee the gun-room. And you leave my sense alone.

*S.* You can stand there till Michaelmas if you've a mind to, Thomas, but you'll not get the better of me. When I say the coach-house, I mean it.

[ 59 ]

*T.* I daresay there never was a more obstinate woman than you.

*S.* That I'm not. But I've got a pride for my house, and I won't have your old rooks making it the way they do. It's disgusting.

*T.* That's it. Tell me I'm disgusting.

*S.* I didn't. I said rooks.

*T.* I know. I'm disgusting.

*S.* Have done talking nonsense. You're not. Call Coles and have those birds put in the coach-house.

Coles was one of the older farm-hands. I once ventured upon the pleasantry of calling him Coke. He remarked that I had a good nerve to be making jokes at the expense of other people's names. It was the first time that it occurred to me that my own was an odd one.

Uncle Thomas, in fact, put up a longer fight than that, but always with the same result. Coles was called, the coach-house it was. Like his brother, my Grandfather, Uncle Thomas was tall, in the six-foot class, with a round face and side-whiskers. He might have been a Crimean general, but he wasn't much of a general when Aunt Sarah was about. She was little and bird-like and competent; she was amiable too, but she was never at a loss to know a coach-house from a gun-room.

By the time the dispute was settled, shooting was

mostly coming to an end. Some of the party drove away to get home before dark, others stayed on. Earlier in the day, some of the birds had been sent in to the kitchen, and presently there was voluble concord at a supper of rook-pie, suitably garnished until the port was on the table, and the room began to cloud with the fumes of near a dozen church-warden clays, at which point I retired to bed.

## XI

AND then there was the partridge-shooting. Punctually on the first of September, the Piddington farm was shot by a party organised by Tom Brown of Wood Eaton, and I was always allowed to carry birds. There was no nonsense about beaters or such high-flown ways. It was a matter of walking the stubble and turnips, and twenty brace with a few hares and landrail was a good day for six guns. There had been a time when my Father was included in these outings, until one day he let his gun off by accident while getting through a hedge, after which his attendance was discouraged. His was, indeed, a somewhat chequered career as sportsman and athlete. I have his cup, won in 1868 at Magdalen College School, for the high jump, long jump, and throwing the cricket ball. Subsequently at Merton, where he was a Post Master, he was No. 2 in the Scratch Four of 1872, but he always told me that he secured his thwart only because no one else of any kind was available, and on the strict understanding that he was not to put his oar in the water. But he was a good sprinter, and took ten and a fifth for the hundred in a year when there were two men up who did it in evens.

I believe game dogs run to considerable variety, what with setters, pointers, retrievers, Labradors and the rest. But as I remember the Piddington shoots, each man had his liver-and-white spaniel. Headquarters on these occasions were not at Uncle Thomas's, but at Aunt Lizzie's, the widow of yet another of my Grandfather's brothers, Charles, who had died young and, I think, without children. Her house is associated in my mind with partridge-shooting and singing 'Abide with Me' in the parlour on Sunday evenings. On the first of September, the guns made an early start from her gate, and walked the Ludgershall fields until lunch time. There is, perhaps, nothing in English weather quite so invigorating as a fine September morning, with a bite in the air and a touch of rust on the foliage. The landscape then is rich in the tones, quiet, crisp, and exquisitely massed, that once made English water-colour the loveliest of national arts. A five-barred gate on a September morning, with wisps of wheat or barley clinging to the hedge alongside, and the glint of stubble beyond, always seems waiting to be drawn by Thomas Girtin or Peter de Wint, or even by some lesser man, a Henry Ninham or John Absalon.

It was, I am sure, those early Oxfordshire days

[ 63 ]

that prepared me for my life-long delight in these gentle and scrupulous artists. What an adorable lot they were, so incorruptible in vision, so direct and austere in statement. And how worthily did the smaller talents honour the tradition that was made glorious by Cotman and Turner (the earlier Turner), and Cox (the earlier Cox) and J. R. Cozens. How dare Mr. Finberg, in his preoccupation with the giants, dismiss John Varley as 'a facile systematiser' and find nothing better than a 'servile and mechanical spirit' in Samuel Prout? Somewhere in the middle of last century the art began to go wrong, getting hot and fussy, with illicit purple longings, but from the days of old Paul Sandby down to the time when David Cox was forgetting his early purity of manner, the school was fitter than most things for English pride. And yet, so unaccountable is taste, fresh and glowing little examples of its genius may still be purchased for a sovereign or so apiece.

All of which has more to do with partridge-shooting than might be supposed. It is the time of roots and fresh haystacks and loaded barns, recorded so repeatedly in the full transparent washes of which those old fellows had an unequalled mastery. Tom Brown and his guests, in cloth leggings, cord breeches, square-bottomed coats of snuff or pepper-and-salt, and low-crowned billy-cocks or tweed glengarrys, lining up across the first ploughland with their spaniels at heel and the September sun glancing off the burnished barrels of their guns, were the right figures in the right scene to set all Cotman's faculties agog.

Lunch was taken in the field, and early autumn lends a fine zest to the appetite. Even the young men of that farming stock seemed to have a capacity for sleep at odd moments by day, and half an hour's grace for a nap after lunch was allowed for those who had a mind to it. There was one George Cave (not, I think, anything to do with Cave of the High School) who at such a time was lying on his back and snoring open-mouthed. Mischievously encouraged by the others, I poured the remains of a beer-bottle down his throat. He was a powerfully built man, and properly decided that I needed teaching, but I had too good a start. His composure, however, was seriously ruffled. He was the crack shot of the party, indeed one of the best in the county. Immediately after lunch, he almost trod on a large French partridge. The flushed bird went straight away from him as he missed it with right and left. He was very displeased with me.

A few weeks ago, in this year 1930, I was passing through Bicester on market-day, and stopped to walk round the town. Thirty-five years had gone by, but

I was sure of the face. 'Excuse me, are you Mr. Cave?' He had been no youth even in the middle 'nineties, and he was an old man now, needing a stick to help him. 'George Cave is my name.' I reminded him of my misdemeanour, and, searching back into his memory, he stood laughing with great satisfaction in Bicester market-place. We talked for a few minutes, and then as we parted, he did a very charming thing: with wholly unaffected courtesy, he thanked me for remembering him. I don't know how manners very well could be gentler than that.

It so happened that, while I was writing this, I spoke of the episode to H. G. Wells, whose ancestry tallies in essentials with my own. Yes, he observed, the middle-classes, braced by a dash of the yeoman, have the best manners in the country. The aristocracy, with many amiable and, when amiable, incomparable exceptions, are arrogant. And the peasantry, again with notable exceptions, are servile. But the yeoman middle-classes, with no secure sense of superiority, and at the same time no cap instinctively to be touched, keep a balance of behaviour never to be neglected. They are alert to manners, treating every contact with a discretion that is always to be observed. 'Thank you for remembering me'—there is a chivalry in that beyond the reach of the overlord and of his serf alike.

# INHERITANCE

I hope that as George Cave went home he too began to think again of the partridge-shooting dinners—not suppers as at rook-shooting—given each year by Aunt Lizzie on the first evening of September. I was considered to have earned a place at table by my day's work, and three or four hares with as many brace of birds on a stick can grow heavy to the shoulder of a slip of thirteen after two or three hours over the rough. I was deeply, but sleepily, sensible of the privilege, and supported myself through the courses only by the necessity of keeping awake for the filberts, for which Aunt Lizzie's garden was famous. Unless the season was very backward, she always gathered the first bushel for this occasion.

## XII

THESE things have no chronological exactitude in my mind. They belong mostly to a period later than my earliest Oxford schooldays, to a time, I suppose, between the ages of twelve and fifteen. And in retrospect a notable feature of those impressionable years is that during them nobody seems to have made the smallest effort to impress me with anything. No: two reservations must be made. H. G. Belcher, in his rather ferocious way, did, I believe, try to make me realise that the mind has its own courses to determine. He said unexpected things, challenged incipient superstitions. He once spoke to me critically of the school management. There was no venom in what he said, nor did he invite my assent. But the fact that such authority could be questioned, opened up speculative vistas hitherto unsuspected.

My other oracle was one Murray, a son of the great Dictionary Murray, whose majestic beard I always associated with the only Latin tag that I could ever keep in my mind:

*Senex promissa barba, horrenti capillo.*

The author, age 10, 16, and 12.

The author, age 16, 18, and 22.

My friend was very long, and once beat me by two inches in the high jump. He strove earnestly to communicate to me his own passion for astronomy, and for a time succeeded. On favourable nights I frequented the Murray garden, approached through a room strewn with tropic profusions of the English language. The heavens were charted for me in a subdued voice of missionary zeal, and it was from Murray that I learnt all that I still know of starry nomenclature. He revealed the Milky Way, and showed me how to fix the Pole Star by the pointers of the Great Bear. I was further made free of Cassiopeia, Orion's Belt, and the Pleiades. I liked particularly the Pleiades, because I discovered that you can see them best by looking at them not direct but a few yards to one side or the other. Altogether it was a little learning, but a pleasant thing, that has remained with me. I am still grateful to Murray for his patient ardour. It might have found an apter pupil, but it was, I like to think, not quite wasted.

Of scholarship at school I acquired none. I am quite prepared to believe that the education was not the less good for me—the mind was no doubt organised by means of instruction the nature of which it has long since forgotten. But searching back now into those days I can recall the particulars of no lesson, not even of any subject, that I was taught.

[ 69 ]

The simplest elements of algebra, euclid, Latin prose, and Doctor Syntax have long since and for ever escaped me. On the other hand, accumulating experience has never driven out of mind a host of little memories that might have been fugitive enough, but have been sharp and durable through years crowded with occasion. I remember—and so intimately that the memories almost become beliefs, as one might say, not I remember but I believe in— such oddly sorted things as these. And yet, perhaps, not so oddly sorted, all indicating at least aspects of a disposition that was moulding into character. In any case I remember:

The duck-decoy at Boarstall, not so much in itself as the knowledge that it was a few meadows away. The left-handed catch at long slip low down by my ankle, on the Abingdon Grammar School field, for which I got my colours. Also two goals scored at home when playing centre-forward against Thames Grammar School. The first was a wretched, scratchy affair, along the ground, a gift of the goal-keeper; but the other was the real thing, well into the upper corner of the net, and I can still hear Andrews II, the inside right, saying 'That's better.' Surely a very strange waif of an event to survive the turmoil of five-and-thirty years. I remember waking in the early hours of the first Monday after the first Sunday

after the first of September, the day appointed
for the opening of St. Giles's Fair, and hearing
the race of caravans down the Woodstock Road
from the city boundary on the stroke of six, as
they roared along in rivalry for the best pitches
on the fair-ground. A farm boy diving into a
horse-pond when we were bathing, and coming
up with his head thickly plastered with black
mud. Catching a fledgling moorhen in the middle of
a field, and asking it why it was unable to fly. I also
once picked a swift up in the garden, where it had
got wing-logged on the grass. The moorhen was
much displeased with me and bit my finger; when
I put it into the water, it dived, and although I
watched for a long time I could not see it come to
the surface again. But moorhens are very cunning
birds, for all their impudence. I remember thinking
always what a lovely name Bablockhythe was, long
before I found out that Matthew Arnold had
thought it lovely too. A girl in a house where I was
staying for holidays, just old enough to have her
hair up; one day when we were alone together, she
let it down suddenly, and kissed me. I was then fifteen, and although I was greatly startled, I thought
it was rather nice. Acting one of my Father's plays,
*The Legend of Vandale*, with my cousins George
and Ruth Drinkwater, and being so busy with the

[ 71 ]

production that I overlooked the necessity of learning my part. Going up into the attic at Boarstall in
the moonlight, and seeing the apples laid out on the
floor. Twenty years afterwards I made these 'Moonlit Apples' into a poem:

At the top of the house the apples are laid in rows,
And the skylight lets the moonlight in, and those
Apples are deep-sea apples of green. There goes
    A cloud on the moon in the autumn night.

A mouse in the wainscot scratches, and scratches, and
    then
There is no sound at the top of the house of men
Or mice; and the cloud is blown, and the moon again
    Dapples the apples with deep-sea light.

They are lying in rows there, under the gloomy
    beams,
On the sagging floor; they gather the silver streams
Out of the moon, those moonlit apples of dreams,
    And quiet is the steep stair under.

In the corridors under there is nothing but sleep.
And stiller than ever on orchard boughs they keep
Tryst with the moon, and deep is the silence, deep
    On moon-washed apples of wonder.

I remember the peculiar damp odour of Parson's
Pleasure, where we used to bathe in the Cherwell.
It impressed me with a vague sense of difference be-
tween water that is damp and water that is wet. I

remember falling out of a willow, up which I had climbed for some starling's eggs, face foremost into a bed of stinging nettles. I remember, too, a remarkable instance of the efficacy of prayer. I was practising in the Winchester Road garden for the school sports, and was dissatisfied with my performance at the high jump. After repeated failures to clear the desired height, I retired into a quiet corner, and devoutly requested God to make me jump one more inch, which He did. It was in the same garden that my sister, playing cricket, excited me to fury by stopping in the middle of a critical run to pick a daisy, and getting run out in consequence.

Another cricket occasion was yet more disturbing. I was playing for the school at Cowley, three miles or so from home. We finished early, and I had a tram-fare into Oxford, walking the rest of the journey to Winchester Road, where I arrived soon after six for tea. But Disciplinarian saw me come in, and detected what I myself had painfully discovered only a few minutes before reaching home. 'Where are your cricket boots?' They were at Cowley. Then I must go and fetch them. After tea? No, before tea. And so, having no further tram-fares, I walked to Cowley and back before tea. Since when, I am glad to say, I have never left any boots at Cowley.

# XIII

ALTHOUGH democracy in our time may be smoothing out class-distinctions, the surprising thing is the pertinacity with which they have survived. I am not at all sure that even now there is any authentic evidence of their decline. Opportunities for achieving wealth and position are much more evenly distributed than they were, but the people who are able to profit by them still assert a class-ascendency of their own. Democratic opportunity has never been so generally exploited as it is in the modern United States of America. There, indeed, anybody may become anything. But I do not find that the American who has become President of his Federal Bank is in the habit of dining with the American who has only become the ice-cart man at his door.

The son of the ice-cart man, it is true, may become President of the United States when the banker's son may be delivering ice to the White House. But these rapid fluctuations of fortune have always been a condition—one might say a prevalent condition,—of society. Clear-cut class-distinction has been a cardinal feature of English life since the

Conquest, probably since Canute or Stonehenge. But this imperturbable class-stability has never had any serious influence upon the stability of families. The classes have remained fixed, but there is hardly a family in the country that in the course of three or four centuries has not drifted about from one class to another. In the very few cases where a family has kept steadily in one class through many successive generations, the explanation is nearly always to be found in the unbroken tenure of a family house. An ancestral home, and in a smaller degree an ancestral business, have been the only secure stabilisers of family rank in English life.

Without these, a family inevitably rises or falls in the social scale. And even with them, the stability operates only on those members of the family who have direct contact with the life of the house or business. So that even families which can boast a class-continuity of centuries, are certainly represented freely in every other class of the community. The serenest of noble houses has connections, if it but knew of them, that would scarcely be admitted to the servants' hall. In the days of full quivers, rank was hard put to it to make ample provision all round, and hardly a generation would pass but what, when elder sons and younger sons had been placed, some undowered daughter would get married off to any man who offered a tolerable match, or even less. Their children in turn would make yet wider excursions, until between yeoman blood and noble blood there ran ceaseless currents of kinship. And still the class-tradition remained.

I wonder what adventures of this nature befell my own family in Piddington. For one thing, it is so difficult to tell how many lives of one breed go to the making of a century. I remember a celebrated Midland figure who lived on in Birmingham to a great age. He could remember in his childhood an old family nurse who could remember her grandfather; and he as a little boy had climbed the hill behind Bewdley to hear the guns at the battle of Worcester in 1650. One life only between the man I knew and the boy who was within earshot of Cromwell's 'crowning mercy.'

Failing such lucky tales, continuity of any kind through the years is strangely hard to trace. Records of any but famous descents perish so swiftly and so finally. I have a passion for writing scraps of history on my possessions, having realised the scarcity of material when one comes to tell of any but official or aristocratic or royal affairs. Looking for some information about my own Drinkwater ancestors in Oxford, I went to search the records of inn licensees in that city; there were none extant earlier than

1905. And so, desiring to set down for my Penelope Ann, who is not yet two, something beyond my own memory of those Piddington folk from whom she comes, folk who have always filled my own consciousness with a deep insistency, I find but a few strays of fact to feed the imagination.

My Great-grandfather Brown came to Piddington from Standlake, also in Oxfordshire, in Waterloo year, 1815. He was then a widower with three daughters, and took the Manor Farm at the top of the village. 'Down-town,' as they chose to speak of the bottom end of the street, was a family of Becks, who had settled there in 1672, the year when Samuel Pepys was compelled to produce a certificate from three ministers of the Church of England that he was innocent of papist guile. The newcomer courted one of the Beck girls, and married her. At the Manor Farm she bore him a second family, among them Uncle Thomas and my Grandfather, John Beck Brown, my Mother's father. Thomas, as I have told, was farming the Manor holding in my own schooldays; and the old name survived in my Mother's, Annie Beck Brown.

These venerable men of my remembrance were yeomen, substantial and of standing, but yeomen unquestionably. Yet they had a bearing that had not risen from the cottage to the farm. I can recover no archives of the Becks of Piddington. Farmers they must have been, since their house was not of the landed gentry type, and in Piddington there was no other alternative. Nor has that part of the world ever run to farms of large dimensions. Small farmers, therefore, but established by straight tenure in one house for a century and a half. This denotes a stamina that could be derived only from somewhat spirited antecedents. Thomas and John Beck walked with a patriarchal, even with a patrician step. I suspect that Brown, the immigrant from Standlake, married, not above his manners, but above his degree, and that his children renewed a Beck ancestry from one of those undowered daughters. Or perhaps the line was begotten at some harvest-moon when class-distinctions were suspended. Awkward and confusing as it may be for the moralists, the honours of breed are by no means the prerogative of legitimacy.

Mrs. Brown (née Beck) of Piddington, and her sons.

# XIV

THESE Browns, I am persuaded, were a fine lot of people. And yet there was in the race a certain inconclusiveness. They had manners, and courage, and wits, but, unless it were harvest-moon, they kept the devil very prudently at arm's length. My Grandfather Brown hated Gladstone, loved cricket, and surprised his fellow tradesmen by reading history, but he was always Mr. Brown who arrived at his Cornmarket shop punctually at 9 A.M. His precision took him to no commercial eminence, but in a modest way it commanded the respect of the citizens of Oxford. John Brown was good for his rates and, if he went to church only on second Sundays, he was on conforming terms with the vicar. In his heart, he mistrusted the establishment, and once privately, in the Water Eaton meadows, said a disrespectful word to his grandson about a Bishop. But otherwise he kept these things hid.

I loved them; literally that. To my childhood, the Browns of Oxfordshire were the only living revelation of good. I knew them intimately, and towards them I conceived a gratitude that has remained with me always. And yet in some way which I could not define, of which indeed at the time I was hardly conscious, I was drawn by a deeper affinity towards the other line of my forebears, the Drinkwaters. Leaving my Father out of the reckoning, affection had nothing to do with it. I did not even know them. My Grandfather Drinkwater and his brother were dead before I was born, and I can only just remember his widow as a very upstanding old lady, heavily gowned in black brocade and velvet, at Leamington. Contacts with my Brown ancestry were many, those with this other, none. And yet the pull of the Drinkwater strain was the stronger, and as the years went by its domination grew. Here was a force that overbade the claims of personal intimacies and affections. I have never been in any doubt as to what was meant by the call of the blood.

There is an agreeable tea-table diversion, which is to speculate on your several choices from the past of some figure whom you would most desire to have known. For me, my Grandfather, George Drinkwater, has no rival. He was born in 1808. I have a painting of him at the age of thirty or so by an unknown artist. One could not wish for pleasanter eyes or a firmer set of the mouth. In the neck-cloth and linen and effectively barbered hair, there are signs, too, of fastidious habits; a little bit of a dandy, per-

George Drinkwater, of Oxford, with his sons, Albert Edwin and Harry George Walter.

haps, in a quiet way. Thus he might have appeared in London, a well-groomed young countryman up from the midlands for Victoria's coronation.

But it is his portrait in old age, a photograph this one, that makes me want to have known him. It is taken with his two sons, and shows a countenance of as right English oak as ever I beheld. It is a face tried but undefeated by experience, with humour glancing behind its grave yet easy dignity. The hair is as ample as ever, as well kept, and hardly iron grey. I do not know whether anything but chance decides these things; but my Mother's hair was white at thirty and my Father's quite unthinned and almost black when he died at seventy-two. The photograph of my Grandfather must have been taken not long before his death in 1873; already he looks his sixty-five years. On the day of her birth, Penelope Ann's resemblance to this portrait provided a startling and ridiculous example of family likeness.

During the nineteenth century the Drinkwaters of Warwickshire and Oxfordshire were farmers, publicans, post-coachmen, and coach proprietors. They were a sturdy lot. The age on five mourning-cards that I have before me averages seventy-eight. They drove hard, rode hard, drank with liberal discretion, went out on to the roads, and sometimes got as far as Paris on no business in particular. They were a much more restless, adventurous people than the Browns, for whom the journey from their farms to the market town was an event. Before telling what I know about these Drinkwaters there are a few things to set down about a remoter, and more speculative ancestry.

A John Drinkwater appears in the Hundred Rolls of Stotterden, Salop, in 1273, a Richard Drynkwater in the Parliamentary Writs of 1309, and I have a Latin parchment of 1390 appointing Johannes Drynkewater attorney for one Agnes Hobbes. From these early days the family flourished in Lancashire and Cheshire, and in the middle of the sixteenth century there are records of a branch that seems to have flourished less, further south, chiefly in the Oxfordshire villages of Tackley and Eynsham. This was my stock. There was a Katherine Drinkwater who made a will at Tackley in 1570. The connections are now obscure, but there is no doubt that they existed. There is now no means of knowing whether Cheshire or Oxfordshire should be credited with the following entry in the minutes of the Royal Society under date July 11, 1678, sixteen years after its foundation:

'Mr. Hooke mentioned the odd effects that were wrought upon the children of a poor woman, who used to gather physical herbs for Mr. Drinkwater, by eating some henbane, which they had mistaken for parsnips: that they all fell stark-mad, but were cured in some short time by the said Mr. Drinkwater, by the taking of alexipharmics and sweating.'

This, I surmise, was the same Mr. Drinkwater who dispensed a curative draught from his pharmacy in Fleet Street during the plague of 1666.

But there is another Drinkwater, also John, of whom more extended notice must be taken. He, too, was of the Cheshire-Lancashire hierarchy, but it pleases me to claim a kinship that no one can dispute.

## XV

FOR many years I came across a frequent entry in my second-hand book catalogues: 'Drinkwater, John. A History of the Late Siege of Gibraltar. London. 1785.' It was not until 1915 that I was tempted to buy a copy of this first edition, a handsome quarto embellished with a fine series of folding plates. Even then it remained unread for some years on my shelves, until I fulfilled an old promise to myself that domestic piety should some day be served. I have no doubt but that the Heralds could help me out in my pretensions; I should like to think that he was some kind of an uncle to me, for he was a very attractive fellow.

This John Drinkwater was born in 1762, at Latchford, in the county of Lancashire, where his family had been founded eight generations earlier, at the end of the sixteenth century, by one Peter Drinkwater. He was educated at the Manchester Grammar School, and at the age of sixteen became an ensign in the Manchester Royal Volunteers. A year later he left for Gibraltar, and was present as a captain during the four years' siege of 1779-1783.

He subsequently held sundry military posts of consequence, refused a knighthood and an offer of the Under-Secretaryship for War, and lived to be over eighty. The D.N.B. states that he was comptroller of army accounts for 1811-1835, but I have a receipt signed by him in that capacity and dated 1800. Late in life he assumed the name of Bethune, for family reasons; the late Sir Edward Cecil Bethune, Director-General of Territorial Forces, 1912-1917, was his grandson.

John was given to history. He published a narrative of the Battle of St. Vincent, which was notable as drawing public attention for the first time to Nelson's meritable service in that engagement; he wrote also on the proceedings at Toulon in 1793; and in 1830 he appeared as the author of nothing less than a *Compendium of the Regent's Canal*. One at least of his seven children inherited his fancy for the pen. John Elliot Drinkwater, so named after his father's chief, General Eliott, published in 1835 a verse translation of Schiller's *Maid of Orleans*. Some verses written in an album in 1828, just after he had been called to the bar, reach a fair level of current University wit:

They dizened me out from the heels to the crown.
They gave me a wig, and they gave me a gown . . .

[ 85 ]

They bade me put on a penitent air,
And they led me into the Hall to swear . . .
The Benchers stood around the table
As well as the poor old souls were able . . .
First, you shall swear to be faithful and true
To the King of England and Scotland too,
Of Ireland and Wales in law and in deed,
And the town of Berwick upon Tweed;
Swear that you never will seek to slaughter,
Himself, his queen, his son or his daughter,
Nor aid nor abet, nor nourish, nor lodge any
Who seek to dethrone with him or his progeny . . .
Next quoth the Clerk, I humbly hope
You will not object to renounce the Pope:
Abjure the belief he has power to pardon all
Crimes, by his bull, or his legate, or cardinal:
For, unless you swear, I cannot acquit you all
Of a hankering after his Romish ritual . . .
Lastly, quoth he, you must utter a ban over
All princes save those of the House of Hanover . . .
And own as your Kings, till the family fail,
Her heirs of the body in protestant tail . . .

Another poem, dated Westminster 1808, and signed
John Drinkwater, cannot have been by John Elliot,
who was then only eight years old. It commemorates
the death of Sir John Moore, and may well have been
by the historian himself in honour of an old comrade-
in-arms. If so, it has a curious negative interest. It
is a poor thing, not even up to John Elliot's stand-

ard. As we shall see, old John was no mean performer at prose; and it may often be observed that
men of whom this is true go all to pieces in verse.

> Hark! the loud trumpet, from Iberia's shore,
> The thund'ring cannon sounds, the rattling car;
> The Muse in anguish mourns the death of Moore;
> And echo, sighing, marks the woes of war.
>
> .   .   .   .   .   .   .
>
> With glory rob'd, with honour's wounds he died;
> In vict'ry's arms the hero sank to rest;
> Thus with his last and falt'ring voice, he cried,
> 'If England's satisfied, in death I'm blest.'

Many soldiers have written verse as bad as that, but
then not many soldiers have written a *Siege of Gibraltar*.

Another of John's sons, Charles Ramsay, became
an admiral, and the father of the Sir Edward
Bethune aforesaid. I have a copy of the Toulon
pamphlet, inscribed 'to Charles Ramsay Drinkwater
from his affectionate Father, Feby. 14, 1823.'

The *Siege* was published when its author was still
only twenty-three. The story of Spain's prolonged
assault, of the garrison's heroic resistance under
Eliott, and of the final triumph of English arms
and policy through the agency of Howe's fleet are
a part of English history. The naval and military
detail of those interminable years is told by Drink-

water with a profusion that is often as tedious as must have been the siege itself. If any expert should trouble to read the book he would, I have no doubt, pronounce it a minor military classic. But to the lay reader, a monotony settles upon these bombarding exchanges after the third month or so, and after the third year the words are no longer capable of performing their duty. If this were all, our classic would be not only unread, but unreadable. Happily, it is not all. The young captain was terribly conscientious in recording the business of the increasingly dreary day, and we very soon learn to take the minutes as read. And then, on every fourth page or so, he enlivens his narrative with an anecdote, a fact, an observation, that sends us confidently forward in the hope of yet more good things to come. It is an anthology of these good things that I propose to submit to my readers, none of whom is ever likely to attempt the selection for himself.

# XVI

THE Gibraltar garrison, which when the siege began was some five thousand strong, was commanded by the General George Augustus Eliott whose name may still sometimes be seen adorning a house of public refreshment by the wayside. Drinkwater, who afterwards became his secretary, gives an engaging picture of him in the history. The General was over sixty when he was shut in on the Rock by the Spaniards, and for nearly four years he preserved discipline, good temper, and efficiency in his forces. During the whole period there were less than fifty desertions, and strangely enough nearly as many malcontents came over from the enemy, though, as Drinkwater observes, it is difficult to know 'what these unhappy men could expect in a confined and blockaded garrison,' that was itself known to be in extreme distress. Many of the unfortunate men who tried to get away from the Rock were dashed to pieces in the descent, and it is not until towards the end of the siege that we read of one 'whose body was exposed as a public spectacle, to intimidate others from provoking a similar fate.'

Even in the essential discipline of food distribution, Eliott was as moderate as firmness would allow. Six months of the siege had passed before he permitted an exemplary punishment for theft. When the scarcity of provisions was such that breadcrumbs were sold at a shilling a pound, milk-and-water at one and threepence a pint, a cow at fifty pounds—with a reservation to the vendor of a pint of milk daily—and onions at half a crown a pound, the General steadily refused to avail himself of any special privileges. In August 1782 the Duc de Crillon, who was in command of the besiegers, sent Eliott a present of game and ice. 'A thousand thanks' were returned, and a civil intimation that in future 'I cannot convert your presents to my own private use,' as 'I confess I make it a point of honour to partake both of plenty and scarcity in common with the lowest of my brave fellow soldiers.' This was the man who, before a night sortie of capital importance, summoned all the officers concerned, and 'lest some matters might have escaped him in the multiplicity of arrangements, desired every person to propose, without restraint, whatever would, in their opinion, further promote the success of the enterprise.' After this engagement—a desperate one—a soldier appeared before him to announce that he had lost his kilt in the attack, and was told by the

General that he might have a commission instead. Eliott's men, not surprisingly, worshipped him. Only once during the siege was any petition presented to him, and that was on a matter of pay which was beyond his jurisdiction. 'The prayer,' which was to be laid 'with all humility at his Majesty's feet,' was not deemed by his Majesty to be worthy of notice.

Once or twice the troops were tried beyond bearing by the exactions of 'mercenary hucksters and liquor dealers' in the town. They ran amok, seizing large quantities of spirit and barricading themselves against their officers. Even then Eliott was very slow to anger. He knew what provocation had caused the trouble. He had faith in his men, and blamed the traders rather than their dupes. Drinkwater saw a party of soldiers roasting a pig by a fire made of cinnamon. The General knew very well how to take the measure of such misbehaviour. A day or two later he might have watched the same men defending a position behind traverses made of casks of flour. As soon as the casks were pierced by the enemy's shot, 'the contents were scooped out and fried into pancakes.'

As the siege wore on and conditions grew worse, Eliott's temper was unruffled. He refused to be discouraged, and good luck generally followed bad to justify him. An epidemic of scurvy, caused by a prolonged diet of salt cod, was relieved by the chance capture of a Dutch cargo of oranges and lemons. 'The salutary effects,' says our historian, 'were almost instantaneous.' The surplus juice was preserved by a lacing of brandy, 'which kept it in so wholesome a state, that several casks were opened in good condition at the end of the siege.' The garrison was also at one time scourged by 'a species of influenza,' of which the 'symptoms were sudden pains, accompanied with a dizziness in the head.' They learnt, however, that the outbreak was 'universal over Europe,' and 'bleeding and a night's rest' usually effected a recovery.

The bombardment of the Rock, we are told, varied greatly in intensity. Often it was extremely violent, and would then subside for weeks together. At one period it consisted of a regular three shells daily, which the defenders profanely saluted as the Father, Son, and Holy Ghost. Towards the end of the siege, as the pressure increased, the routine of the garrison was tightened up. 'As affairs were becoming daily more interesting,' the Governor 'determined to have no idle hands,' and 'Musicians, who before had been exempted from duty, returned to the use of the firelock and shovel.' By Christmas, 1782, the situation, which Drinkwater had repeatedly remarked as 'interesting,' was becoming 'irksome and vexatious,' but in January 1783 Howe defeated the Spaniards at sea, the siege was raised after an investment lasting over three years and seven months, and Gibraltar was declared to remain a British possession.

Captain Drinkwater—he became Lieutenant-Colonel in 1796—tells his story with no affectation, but with the soundness of style that comes of having something definite to say. As a last example of his manner, the following remarkable account of an early incubator may be given:

'This extreme scarcity of provisions, it may well be imagined, could not fail to exercise the invention of individuals. A singular mode of hatching chickens was about this time successfully practised by the Hanoverians; and, as it may be acceptable to some readers, the process, as communicated by a friend, is here inserted. The eggs were placed, with some cotton, wool, or other warm substance, in a tin case of such construction as to be heated either by a lamp or hot water; and, by a proper attention to the temperature of heat, the eggs were commonly hatched in the usual time of a hen's sitting. A capon (however strange it may appear) was then taught to rear them. To reconcile him to this trust, the feathers were plucked from his breast and belly; he was then gently scourged with a bunch of nettles, and placed upon the young hatch, whose downy warmth afforded such comfort to the bared and smarting parts, that he, from that period, reared them up with the care and tenderness of a mother.'

With which I may take leave of, I would he were, my Uncle John.

## XVII

THIS John was one of the big fellows of Lancashire and Cheshire. I must return to my own kin of the southern Midlands, uncelebrated men and women of whom it has been a matter of difficult patience to recover the fragments of a story. And yet they are fragments, it seems to me, of a kind that is never without interest, even significance; like the scattered strands that we may unearth on the site of some city where nothing more remains to tell us of the ample, intricate life that once was there. A word, a hieroglyph, the rubbed note of a pattern, even no more than the broken curve of a clay pitcher—how much virtue can stir again in these. And so of the scanty chronicles, so scanty, indeed, as to make the term chronicle an audacity, which are all that survive of these, as of so many other millions of obscure lives. Usually, in hardly more than a generation from the grave, they pass out of recollection, wholly and for ever. When we are led, as I have been, to search back into the chill silence of their lost world, we are fortunate to detect here and there the echo of an echo, to surprise the ghost of a ghost. And yet even such fugitive recoveries are made securely from a life definite, eager, three-dimensioned. History may be eloquent in a thumb-print on the margin of a nursery-rhyme.

Here, then, is what I have been able to learn of my Drinkwaters. The first of whom I find any record is Richard, of Tackley in Oxfordshire, who in 1729 married Ann Pembery, on November 3rd. The founding of the family, if we may take it as that, was not all that propriety would demand; in fact, it was flighty, since their first child, Elizabeth, was baptised less than four months after the wedding, on February 18th, following. Nor, it is to be feared, did Elizabeth of her occasion take

More composition and fierce quality,

as her name appears in the burial register for 1732. Richard and Ann, however, did well by their contract, and in 1750 the seventh child was born. The Tackley registers from this date contain some eighty Drinkwater entries; the village has but a population of five hundred. There were many deaths in infancy, and many octogenarians. George, Richard, and John are steadily recurrent names among the men, with an occasional Thomas or Samuel, and once a Valentine, while the generations of Elizabeth, Ann, and Mary are diversified by a Rose, a Lydia, and a

[ 96 ]

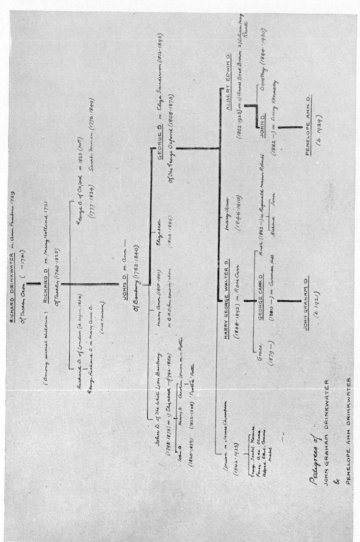

Pedigrees of John Graham Drinkwater and Penelope Ann Drinkwater.

Lætitia. In records elsewhere I have found a Civil Drinkwater among the men, and a Mercy among the women. Rose appears to have touched bottom of the family fortunes. In five years, with no husband, she had three children, two of whom died as infants in the Union Workhouse, and she herself was defeated by the uneven odds at the age of thirty-seven. Three years before the end, the banns of her marriage were published, but they came to nothing, and she died a spinster. Had all been well, it seems, she should have been Mrs. Daniel Dollery.

The men were shepherds and farm-labourers; in the nineteenth century some of them were still not literate beyond making their mark as witnesses. As befitted their pastoral calling, ten Drinkwaters between the years 1766 and 1788 were 'buried in Woollen only,' in conformity with laws passed for the encouragement of the wool staplers. Now and again one of the Tackley labourers rose to a small holding of his own, but such advancement was rare. In 1599, John Drinkwater of Gagingwell, a neighbouring hamlet, was noted in the Eustone burial register as 'formosi peccoris custos'—a keeper of fine cattle, and that, so far as I can discover, was the last flourish made by any Drinkwater on the land. It was not until one or two of them migrated to the near towns of Banbury and Oxford that things looked up a little. When this migration began I am not sure; I fear it was too late for me to claim Jane Drinkwater of St. Ebbs in Oxford who died in 1705 'A Quaker.'

After two daughters, Ann Pembery of Tackley presented her husband Richard with three sons, duly named John, born in 1736, Richard, in 1740, and George, in 1744. This elder Richard died at Tackley in 1781, being 'buried in Woollen only' on November 30th, having eight days before made a will that was proved at Oxford on December 1st. The date of his marriage, 1729, gives him at least a round reckoning of seventy years. His son of the same name, born in 1740, lived to be eighty-five. On May 31, 1761, a few months before he came of age, he married Mary Holland, also of Tackley, as witnessed by Samuel Lemon and Richard Jenkins. They had three sons, again, and in the established order, John, Richard, and George. Of these, Richard, born in 1772, came to London, and, apart from a reference in his brother George's will from which his death before 1834 is established, disappears from my papers. John, however, born in 1763, and George, born in 1777, are less elusive, and it is with them that the coaching history of the family begins.

## XVIII

JOHN, the elder brother, was established in Banbury before the turn of the century, since his eldest son and child, my Great-uncle John, was born at The Ark, a farm and malthouse in that town, in 1798. John senior was then thirty-five, an advanced age, according to Tackley standards, for first paternity. His wife was Ann. At The Ark also were born Mary Ann, in 1801, who lived to be eighty, Elizabeth, in 1803, who lived to be eighty-two, and George, my Grandfather, in 1808. The gap between 1803 and 1808 suggests that the family may have been completed by a Richard unrecorded but demanded by tradition. In those early days a move seems to have been made from The Ark to The Town Hall Tavern. My Great-uncle John, I have been told, remembered going on a milk-round as a boy, but in the first years of the new century his father was thriving modestly with a coach plying between Banbury and Oxford.

The population of Banbury at that time was four thousand. The town had no paving, no lighting, and middens fouled the streets across the mud of which passage had to be made by stepping-stones. Rather less than two hundred years earlier, drunken Barnaby had pilloried Banbury puritanism in one of his most celebrated rhymes:

> In my progresse travelling Northward,
> Taking my farewell o'th Southward,
> To Banbery came I, O prophane one!
> Where I saw a Puritane-one,
> Hanging of his Cat on Monday,
> For killing of a Mouse on Sunday.

Camden in his *Britannia* named the town famous for cheese, and in 1610, finding that Philemon Holland in his English version had taken the liberty of adding cakes and ale, he amended ale to zeal in consideration for the townsmen. But though zeal was confirmed by Barnaby, ale was as near a shot at the truth, as John of The Ark could testify, and no one of delicate taste would dispute the supremacy of Banbury cakes. These were famous even in the sixteenth century. In 1800, however, Banbury was notable for dirt; also, it would seem, for pride, since

> Dirty Banbury's proud people
> Built a Church without a Steeple.

It was not until 1835 that, under persuasion of the Municipal Reform Act, the town took to sprucer ways.

By the courtesy of Mr. Thomas Loveday, Vice-

INHERITANCE

Chancellor of Bristol University, I am able to print
the following passages from the correspondence of
an ancestor, John Loveday of Williamscot, with his
son Thomas, then an undergraduate at Magdalen
College, Oxford.

'Williamscot,
Friday, July 25, 1806.
. . . I desired John to open whatever letter might
arrive from Oxford this morning; so that he communicated the glorious news [of a University suc-
cess] to good Mr. Rushworth, whose tears of joy
flowed apace, as they have since done here. He ex-
pects you to eat a hot Roll with him to-morrow,
when a Horse will be ready to convey you afterwards
hither. Perhaps you will secure a place this evening
in Drinkwater's Convenience, and sleep for your
own at the Inn, that you may be in readiness for an
early departure to-morrow. . . .
P.S. Drinkwater shall be paid by the Servant for
your fare to-morrow.
[His sister Anne adds a note of felicitation, and
'Your brothers are just setting out for Farnboro
for a Cricket Match, which the weather does not
favour.']

'Williamscot,
Whitmonday, 1807.
. . . You will now receive a £10 Note, which you
will account for when we meet. . . . It was vexatious that my last packet did not reach you till the

Reading coach was gone; especially as Drinkwater engaged that you should have it the night before. [And Thomas will read carefully Archbishop Secker's Sermon on Confirmation before Saturday, when he is to appear at Christ Church to be presented to the Bishop's Chaplain. Also the town of Reading has been misconducting itself politically, and would have done well to follow the example set by the county of Berks.]'

'Williamscot,
Thursday, July 2, 1807.
. . . You act quite right in staying for Mrs. Benwell, and in avoiding the heat and hurry attending Drinkwater. [And John will advise about the cricket-ball, and tell of the feats of yesterday . . . Butcher's Meadow was cleared on Tuesday, as Withy Hold promises to be to-morrow . . . much damaged Hay from both.]'

'Williamscot,
Wednesday, Oct. 7, 1807.
[Receipt for payment of bill to Cooke the bookseller to be sent] with whatever else you may have to send by Drinkwater on Sunday, when White may bring your packet from Banbury.'

'Williamscot,
Saturday, October 24, 1807.
[A present of two Banbury cheeses from his Mother to a friend 'from her own dairy.'] William heard yesterday at Radway that Chambers was returned to

College, so that he will probably be *solus cum solo*
on his journey this afternoon. Drinkwater will not
leave him behind, as you say the Pastor of Finedon
was by his Driver.'

'Williamscot,
Wednesday, Feb. 10, 1808.

. . . You will probably write hither at the end
of the week, when William tells me a parcel will
be ready for me, which I desire may not be sent till
Saturday night to Drinkwater, as John will probably return that day from London, and may have
somewhat to add to it. I must reserve whatever
occurrences for John, whom we have not heard from
since he went to Town; where we hope he has attended the Banbury Committee and Whitelocke
Trial [John Whitelocke, cashiered by Court Martial, 1808, for the disaster at Buenos Ayres].'

Just the echo of an echo here of the 'tin yard,' the
ghost of ghostly wheels. And yet, as Mr. Loveday
tells his son to book a place in Drinkwater's Convenience, there is life again on the Banbury Road.

## XIX

THE heat of Drinkwater's Convenience on a July day of 1806, a day when Charles Fox lay dying in Stable Yard, St. James's, may well be realised; but the hurry is another matter. And yet we to-day who think ourselves excelsior at two hundred miles an hour may pause to recollect that our ancestors of 1800 thought themselves no less at ten. In the year 2000 our two hundred may have dwindled as plaintively, and to as little purpose. At the end of the eighteenth century the Edinburgh Mail was doing the four hundred miles to Lombard Street in forty hours, a speed so alarming that a peer of the realm was advised to break his journey at York, several passengers who had gone through without stopping having 'died of apoplexy from the rapidity of the motion.' To Thomas Loveday of Magdalen, John Drinkwater of The Ark doubtless sent the flints spinning from his iron tyres in a very dare-devil way. These high-speed coaches were already known on the roads as flying-machines.

But John was unpunctual also, we read. The truth is—it being far enough away to tell it—that he had too wide a capacity for Banbury ale. There is a tradition in the family that he lived to be a very cantankerous old fellow. I possess an odd emblem of his humours. Once he drank an evening through with his cronies, who in a crescendo of larking cut all the silver buttons from his dress coaching coat. Though not precisely all, since they overlooked the ornamental couple behind, a survival of the old fashion of tail-looping. These were retrieved by the family, and handed down as heirlooms. I have them before me as I write, their engraved J. D.'s still showing clearly in an elegant script.

Relating this festive incident to H. G. Wells, I heard from him of a great-grand-uncle of his own who also, and more cataclysmically, adventured in the coaching line. He, it seems, drove foursome between Chichester and Midhurst. In 1810, setting out on his night journey, he had done too well by the cordials of his inn, and took the wrong turning. With no passengers that stage, he deployed in his cups down a by-lane, and drove his team into the canal quay; where, with four good greys, he was drowned.

John of The Ark and Town Hall Taverns drank his ale and kept his Convenience on the road, though at uncertain hours, but made no great stir in the world. Attending none too strictly to business, he died in 1840, at the age of seventy-seven of 'Mortification of Thigh from fracture produced by his accidentally falling down.' Stubborn, we make take it, if not virtuous, to the end. But in the meanwhile his brother George, fourteen years his junior, had been laying firmer foundations in Oxford.

John of The Ark had several children; his brother George had none. But George at Oxford achieved a stability that was a timely support to the improvidence of Banbury. The second son of Banbury, George (unless there was an intermediate Richard, to make him the third), was born, as we have seen, in 1808. September 9th was the date. In 1823 he was, at the age of fifteen, passive party to a contract of which the terms are of sufficient interest to set out, and read, in full.

'This Indenture Witnesseth [a prettily incised Indenture it is, as nice an example of "the one part" as could be desired] That George Drinkwater Son of John Drinkwater of Banbury in the County of Oxford with the consent of his Uncle George Drinkwater of Oxford Coachmaster doth put himself Apprentice to William Shackleford of the City of Oxford Coachmaker to learn his Art and with him after the manner of an Apprentice to serve from the twenty-first day of September now last past unto the full End and Term of Seven Years from thence next following to be fully complete and ended During which Term the said Apprentice his Master faithfully shall serve his secrets keep his lawful command every where gladly do He shall do no damage to his said Master nor see to be done of others but to his Power shall tell or forthwith give warning to his said Master of the same He shall not waste the goods of his said Master nor lend them unlawfully to any He shall not commit fornication nor contract Matrimony within the Said Term He shall not play at cards or Dice Tables or any other unlawful Games whereby his said Master may have any loss with his own goods or others during the said Term without Licence of his said Master He shall neither buy nor sell He shall not haunt Taverns or Playhouses nor absent himself from his said Master's service day or night unlawfully But in all things as a faithful Apprentice He shall behave himself towards his said Master and all his during the said Term And the said William Shackleford in consideration of the sum of forty-two pounds of lawfull money to him in hand paid by the said George Drinkwater the Uncle party hereto the receipt whereof he doth hereby acknowledge his said Apprentice in the Art of a Coach Painter which he useth by the best means that he can shall teach and instruct or cause to be taught or instructed Finding unto the said Apprentice sufficient Meat Drink and Washing and Lodging during the said Term and the said George Drinkwater party hereto doth covenant and agree to find the said George Drinkwater the Apprentice sufficient Clothes and all other necessaries during the said Term And for the true performance of all and every the said Covenants and Agreements either of the said Parties bindeth himself unto the other by these Presents In witness whereof the Parties above named to these Indentures have put their Hands and Seals the fifteenth day of July and in the fourth year of the Reign of our Sovereign Lord George the fourth by the Grace of God of the United Kingdom of Great Britain and Ireland King Defender of the Faith and in the Year of our Lord One Thousand Eight Hundred and Twenty three

     GEORGE DRINKWATER
     GEORGE DRINKWATER Sn[r]
     WM. SHACKLEFORD

Signed Sealed and Delivered
(being first duly stampt)
in the presence of
ROBINSON BARTRAM.'

The document bears a sixpenny and a two-pound stamp and is endorsed with Shackleford's receipt for the stipulated sum of forty-two pounds. The young George Drinkwater's signature is written in a hand well-formed for a boy of fifteen.

His Uncle George, having undertaken this responsibility on July 15th, went considerably farther on the 24th when at the age of forty-six he married Mrs. Sarah Forman of Coach and Horses Lane in the city of Oxford, herself one year his senior. They were married at St. Peters-in-the-East. In *Jackson's Oxford Journal* the bridegroom is described as 'late proprietor of the Banbury Coach.' He had, in fact, thus early in middle age handed on the coaching business to a new generation, and was able to enjoy a comfortable retirement until 1834, on Saturday July 26th of which year the following notice appeared in *Jackson:*

'On Saturday last died, in the 57th year of his age, Mr George Drinkwater, formerly proprietor and driver of the mail coach from Oxford to Banbury. He had for some years retired from business, and lived in this city much respected by all who knew him.'

In the 1830 Poll of Freeholders for Knights of the Shire for the County of Oxford he appears in the Banbury list as a freeholder of that town, resident at Oxford, his tenants being 'Thos. Butler and others.' In his will he is described as George Drinkwater of No. 18 Walton Street, in the Parish of St. Thomas Oxford, Gentleman. He left a life interest in his estate, including the freehold property in Banbury, to his wife, Sarah, and after two legacies of fifty pounds apiece to the son and daughter of his late brother Richard the residuary interest in equal parts to such sons and daughters of his brother John of Banbury as should survive her. Sarah died in 1849 at the age of seventy-three. In her will she appointed her nephew George, the apprentice and my Grandfather, executor to carry out the terms of her late husband's will, and further left him thirty pounds, all her plate, and 'the clock now standing in my kitchen.'

## XX

WHEN my Grandfather was apprenticed by his
Uncle to William Shackleford, his brother John
was already twenty-five, and four years a married
man with two sons, yet another John, and Henry.
His Uncle George retiring from business, and his
father, John of The Ark, being none too enterpris-
ing at sixty, it was he who now became effective
head of the family and its coaching interests, to be
joined later by his younger brother George when
the Shackleford articles were ended. The Oxford-
Banbury stage was extended to Warwick, and the
two brothers defied all competition on that route
until the coaches were finally driven off the roads by
the railways. My Grandfather died in 1873, at the
age of sixty-five, John in 1878, at the age of eighty.

This John, my Great-uncle, was a man at once of
great amiability and character. He was familiar with
coaching ways from infancy. He may well have been
one of the children who would gather at the foot of
Stanmore Hill waiting for the arrival of the Birmingham Mail, while a smartly dressed jockey with
a gilt staff was in readiness with a rosetted spare

horse to help the incoming team up into the town. This spare was known as the cock-horse, which has in imagination the world over been ridden to Banbury Cross.

While still a boy, John became an adept with the ribbons on the box-seat of his father's coach. One winter's day, when he was twenty, among his passengers from Oxford was a pretty girl who reached the journey's end much distressed by cold. He gave her a hot peg of brandy and a Banbury cake, and within a year had married her. She was six years older than he, but they were happy until she died in 1850 at the age of fifty-eight. In 1860, when he was sixty-two, he married again, one Ann Bezley of Bloxam, a widow, but the second venture was not a success. It is said that the lady was not quite the lady she should have been; in any case, she ran away from him, and left him not inconsolable.

I have an oil painting of John, possibly done by the same hand as that of my Grandfather. Whoever the artist was, he had a very pleasing competence, doing his work directly and sanely without making a fuss about it. We recall the passage in *Hawbuck Grange* where Surtees speaks of the picture of Cornelius and Mrs. Cake—'most likely acquired in the usual way of inn-portraiture—some travelling artist

John Drinkwater, of the White Lion, Banbury.

painting for his bill. On no other supposition can we account for the wonderful tendency publicans have to "run the portrait." ' John, by the evidence of our artist, was not so good-looking a man as his brother George, but of a very frank and satisfactory countenance nevertheless. Once in Burford, passing down the village street, I saw the name Drinkwater over a butcher's shop. And there, framed in his open shop-front, with folded arms, was the owner, the living image of John's portrait.

In 1823 John was residing at The George and Dragon in Banbury Horse Fair, and in 1830 at The Flying Horse in Parsons Lane. In the latter year he may have been among the Yeomanry called out to suppress the rioters who were burning the new threshing-machines at Banbury and Chipping Norton. By 1832 he had moved again, this time to The White Lion, one of the principal houses in town, where he stayed until in his later years he retired to his farm at Drayton, two miles out at the junction of the Warwick and Stratford roads.

The White Lion, in High Street, was listed as a commercial inn, posting house and coach office, licensed to sell wine, spirits, and porter. The first note that I have of John's tenancy is a small card, given to me by Mr. Page, the present landlord, which reads:

[ 113 ]

'118
Mr. Drinkwater
   Admit the Bearer to the DINNER on
   Tuesday, the 25th. Sept. 1832.
Dinner on the Table at Four o'Clock.'

An indenture dated 1834, intelligible no doubt to lawyers but not to me, records Mr. John Drinkwater as selling 'All that Capital Messuage in Banbury commonly called or known as the White Lion Inn with the Offices Outbuildings Coachhouses Stables Yards and Gardens thereto belonging,' and much besides, to Mr. John Golby Milward for the sum of five shillings of lawful money current in Great Britain. It further records the same as leasing the same to the same for one year at the rent of a peppercorn, the term to be from the day next before the day of the date of these presents. Doubtless my Grand-uncle was given an English translation of this document, and he seems to have come to no harm by the transaction, since he was, intermittently, landlord of The White Lion until 1865. The most pleasing feature about the ambiguous lease is John's signature at the foot of it, done with a bold flourish in a notably stylish hand.

Once when I was passing through Banbury I stopped for refreshment at The Red Lion. There in

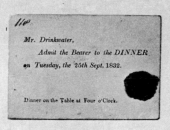

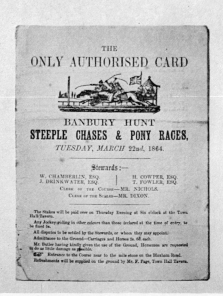

THE

# ONLY AUTHORISED CARD

BANBURY HUNT
## STEEPLE CHASES & PONY RACES,
*TUESDAY, MARCH 22nd, 1864.*

Stewards :—

W. CHAMBERLIN, ESQ.    H. COWPER, ESQ.
J. DRINKWATER, ESQ.    T. FOWLER, ESQ.
CLERK OF THE COURSE—MR. NICHOLS.
CLERK OF THE SCALES—MR. DIXON.

The Stakes will be paid over on Thursday Evening at Six o'clock at the Town Hall Tavern.

Any Jockey riding in other colours than those declared at the time of entry, to be fined 5s.

All disputes to be settled by the Stewards, or whom they may appoint.

Admittance to the Ground—Carriages and Horses 2s. 6d. each.

Mr. Butler having kindly given the use of the Ground, Horsemen are requested to do as little damage as possible.

☞ Entrance to the Course near to the mile stone on the Bloxham Road.

Refreshments will be supplied on the ground by Mr. F. Page, Town Hall Tavern.

John Drinkwater of the White Lion, Banbury. A Dinner
Admission Card, 1832 (*top*), and Race Card, 1864 (*bottom*).

the bar I saw a framed Bill that much excited me.
It read thus:

'The Public are respectfully informed that, for
their better accomodation,

## A NEW POST
## COACH
"The Union Railway,"

Will commence running from the
Red and White Lion
Hotels, Banbury
on
Monday, April the 20th.,

And will continue to do so
Every Afternoon, Sundays Excepted,
At a Quarter-before Three o'Clock,
Thro' Brackley, Buckingham, Winslow,
And Whitchurch, to the
Aylesbury Station,
To meet the seven o'clock train
To London.

Returns from Euston Square at Three o'Clock in
the afternoon; Aylesbury at five; Buckingham at
seven; and Banbury at Nine o'Clock.

Performed by the Public's most obedient Servants
C. W. FOWLER
JOHN DRINKWATER
THOMAS SWAINE

April 11th, 1840
J. G. RUSHER, Printer, Banbury'

[ 115 ]

I thought of trying a bid for possession, but on reflection decided that the Bill properly belonged to the Red Lion, of which my papers told me that C. W. Fowler was proprietor at that date. In 1930, however, I heard that The Red Lion was to be demolished by Mr. Woolworth who has made such a lot of five cents. I was too late for the sale of effects, but by an enquiry from the auctioneer learnt that my Bill had gone to a corn-merchant of Stratford-upon-Avon at seventeen shillings and sixpence. I spent a very hot summer's day trailing him through the markets of Shakespeare's town, and finally brought him to bay in a tap-room over against the Corn Exchange.

It was a Corn Exchange redolent of early boyhood days round about Bicester. Here were displayed the same old boards recommending Corn, Cakes, Seeds and Fertilizers, Artificial Manures, Tarpaulins, Flour Mills and Agricultural Experts. My quarry was familiar of all these, but it was a dull and sultry day and he had retreated to the tap-room across the way. Yes, he had bought the Bill. All the innkeepers of Banbury, however, were eager to acquire it. A local document, he was told, of inestimable value. Four guineas had been offered for it. Two more pints, please, Miss. Very well, let it be four guineas —having driven two hundred and more miles from

Announcing John Drinkwater's new coach, 1840. Stevengraph Silk
Pictures, 'The Good Old Days' and 'The Present Time.'

Cornwall, I was ready to make a deal and have done with it. No; he was convinced that it was worth six guineas if it was worth a pint—two more, please —and so six guineas it was. And if any innkeeper of Banbury wants it now, he may bid fifty and still want.

John became a personage in Banbury. I have— also by the kindness of Mr. Page—'The Only Authorised Card' of the 'Banbury Hunt Steeple Chases and Pony Races' held on Tuesday, March 22, 1864. And here among the Stewards is John Drinkwater, Esq. The Mr. Page of those days was running two matches, one with Hipbriar against Mr. Nichols' Harlequin, one with Artful Dodger against Mr. Butler's Illuminator. The best entry was for The Banbury Stakes, with fourteen runners, while in the United Hunters' Stakes only one horse, Mr. W. Mackenzie's Wigley, went to the post. At the close of the meeting A Scurry Steeple Chase was 'made up on the Ground.'

John Drinkwater had taken his farm at Drayton at least as early as 1854. It was known as Drayton Fields, and it was there that he died in 1878. As he was still proprietor of The White Lion as late as 1868, it is clear that for some years he carried on the double business. My Father remembered spending many weeks with him at Drayton in vacations, and fishing in the Wroxton ponds near by, at the seat of the Norths. Old John of The Ark may well have known George the Third's Lord North, who was member for Banbury: hardly, perhaps, have driven him in his Convenience, since so exalted a personage would have a private coach of his own.

In his later years my Great-uncle John saw coaching dwindle to its last decline, but until he left The White Lion about 1870 there was still enough traffic on the road to keep the splendid old yard busy at all hours. John is remembered by his granddaughter, a cousin euphoniously known in the family as Trottie Potter, to whom I owe many kindnesses and much treasure from the stores of her now long memory. When as a girl she knew her grandfather, he was a name for benevolence. I have a photograph that shows him sitting stiffly, looking out rather severely from between white side-whiskers, dressed in a short frock-coat of fine black face-cloth, white tie, a fancy waistcoat, and light braided trousers.

He then had long given up his place on the box-seat, but was still up early every morning to see the London-Birmingham Mail into the yard and take breakfast with the passengers, allowing himself a pint of beer. But he was a very abstemious man, as was his brother George, my Grandfather. They may have regarded their father's somewhat liberal example as one to be neglected. It was John's custom to take his pint of beer at breakfast, and then nothing till night-time, when he mixed himself a whiskey and water in a silver mug.

He died with a personal estate returned as being under three thousand pounds. In the Administration of his Will, granted to his daughter's executor, he was described as of Drayton Fields, Farmer.

# XXI

John's sister, Mary Ann, who married her cousin, George Richard the son of Richard, dying in 1881, appointed as executors of her will 'John Drinkwater of Banbury in the county of Oxon and Harry George Walter Drinkwater of 8 New Road Oxford, Gentleman.' These were her nephews, John the son of John of The White Lion, and Harry, my Father's brother, the son of George. This John himself died at 31 Church Lane, Banbury, a bachelor, in 1885, aged sixty-five. He appears to have been an amusing fellow, with a notable disinclination to work. However, he left four hundred and twenty-five pounds.

The apprenticeship of my Grandfather George to William Shackleford ended in 1829, within a few days of his twenty-first birthday. Although his trade had been specified in the articles as that of a coach-painter, he no doubt left his seven years in Shackleford's employment with a sound knowledge of the coaching business in general. It would come naturally enough to the son and nephew of the men whose coaches he had known from infancy, halting at the Banbury stage on the Warwick-Oxford road. He had lived among horses ever since he could remember, had often been up on the box before his hands had power to hold a team together, knew the life of the stables and harness-rooms, and could direct the long flexible curl of a coachman's whip to a leader's shoulder before he had grown up. At the age of twenty-one he was ready to take his place in the family business, joining his brother John, ten years older than himself. He became, and for several years continued to be, one of the regular drivers on the Drinkwater stages.

The coaches which I can trace definitely to the family proprietorship were *Novelty*, *The Union Railway*, *The Rival*, *Sovereign* (it later became *The Original Sovereign*), and *Regulator*. In 1831, George Drinkwater is recorded as coachman of the last named, though at this date the owner appears to have been Joseph Hearn; it was advertised as John Drinkwater's in 1846. George Drinkwater on *Regulator* drove 'four browns, through Woodstock, Sturdy's Castle, Deddington, Banbury, and Warwick, Warwick Arms Hotel,' the return journey ending at The Angel in Oxford. Some time later he moved to Warwick, it doubtless being found easier to work the stages with one driver resident in that town. He appears on the Warwick rate-list for 1843, in which year his first child was born, a daughter

Louisa. He had married Eliza or Elizabeth Sanderson, whose family also was in the coaching business. In Warwick three other children were born to them, Harry George Walter, in 1844, Mary Ann, registered as 'daughter of George and Elizabeth Drinkwater Coachman West Street,' in 1846, and Albert Edwin, my Father, in 1852. His house has been demolished, but it stood a few yards away from Bowling Green Street, just opposite a large coaching yard which has also disappeared. It may have afforded cover for *Regulator* at night when the passengers had been dropped at The Warwick Arms.

I am not sure of the identity of *The Rival* and *Sovereign*, though there was a *Sovereign* that ran from Worcester through Pershore, Evesham, Chipping Norton and Woodstock to Oxford, and on through Wycombe and Uxbridge to The Bull-and-Mouth in London. Perhaps the most famous of the Drinkwater coaches was *Novelty*, which worked for many years between Oxford and Banbury. The return journey was done daily, the forty-four miles being covered in four hours. At one time *Novelty* was driven by Dick Bolton, and when *The Oxonian* was put on from the other end of the road in opposition, the rivalry between him and John Vigers, 'a very smart coachman,' became one of the excitements of Banbury gossip. But I think that my

Grandfather, in the days before he went to Warwick and worked only on *Regulator* was sometimes up on the *Novelty* box. I have a whip that suggests this. There is a tradition in the family that old John of The Ark and the silver buttons, drove at one time on the Ross and Hereford road. This points to some association with *Mazeppa*, the Hereford-Ross-Cheltenham-Oxford-London coach, famous throughout the west of England for its coachmen, its guards, and its teams. Well on into the nineteenth century, its arrival at the Roebuck in Oxford at the end of the second stage from Cheltenham, Henry Charlton up, with four bays, was greeted by Richard Gurden, the landlord, in powdered hair and long Hessian boots. Thence John Bramble took the reins with four browns to London. On the return journey, Richard Snowden took the bays to Oxford, no less a personage than Charles Bliss, Esq., the browns to Cheltenham, and Edward Fowles—a 'first-class light-handed coachman that ever took reins in hand'—an unspecified team to Hereford. In this contemporary record there is no mention of the second driver on the Hereford-Cheltenham stage. The family tradition of which I speak is the kind of thing that is nearly always founded on fact, and it is a reasonable surmise that John Drinkwater is the missing name.

[ 123 ]

There is a period during his earlier Banbury days when I cannot trace his movements in that town, and he may very well have gone further west on temporary employment. My whip bears out the conjecture that the *Mazeppa* people in the 'thirties were on terms of old standing with the Drinkwaters. My Grandfather, as I surmise, was at that time an occasional driver of *Novelty*, on days, perhaps, when *Regulator* was taken by his elder brother. *Novelty* took the Kidlington road to Deddington, missing Woodstock; *Mazeppa* from London came into Oxford by Headington and left for Witney. The two roads do not intersect, but *Mazeppa* from The Roebuck in Cornmarket would daily pass *Novelty* from The Mitre in the High. My Father told me that his father was presented with the whip on the twenty-fifth anniversary of this daily meeting at Carfax corner, though George himself was but new in the succession of *Novelty* drivers. On a silver mount there is an inscription, curiously engraved in Gothic type:

APPEZAM

OT

YTLEVON

G. Drinkwater

In Birch Reynardson's *Down the Road* (1875) I came across the following:

[ 124 ]

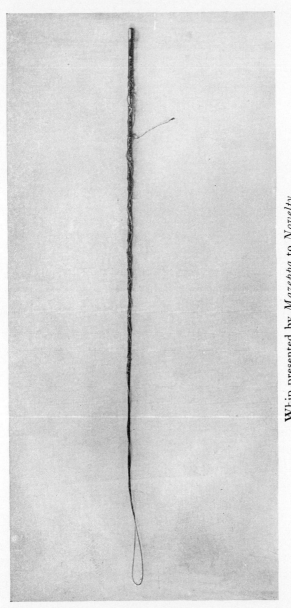

Whip presented by *Mazeppa* to *Novelty*.

'It is laughable to see the length of whip sometimes adopted. This at once denotes a "muff." There
is no use having a whip as tall as the monument,
with a thong as long as Piccadilly; a foot and a
half of thong and point together, hanging below
your hand, gets entangled with your reins and anything else it comes in contact with. Some may say,
"I can't reach my leaders if it's shorter." This is not
a fact; you can if you do it according to Cocker, and
are not what is called a "regular gardener." The
correct length for a whip, according to William
and Joseph Ward of Newington, who are all dead
and gone, was 5 ft. 1½ in. from the end of the butt
to the holder, and for the thong 12 ft. 5 or 6 in. from
the holder to the end of the point; anything more is
superfluous. Rest to their souls; they are all gone,
I trust, with the good niggers. They were the best
whipmakers in the world, as was proved by ninety
out of a hundred coachmen using their whips on
every road in the Kingdom. Almost any saddler,
however small, in towns where a coach passed
through, had them, and I have seen them produced
in bundles to choose from. They were not only first-
rate, but very cheap, compared with the price one
pays in these days; twelve or fourteen shillings
would produce quite a swell whip, and I have bought
really good ones, with plain leather handles, three
for a guinea. These were without ferrules of any
kind, and, if the stick turned out good, were ferruled
afterwards. A whip of the same kind, with brass
ferrules used to cost ten shillings; one with silver

ferrules was hardly known, except on the Lord Mayor's coach, or to drive the judge at the Assizes.'

I took my Grandfather's whip down, and there sure enough was the legend on the handle, in black print:

Will<sup>m</sup> & Jos<sup>h</sup> Ward
Makers
Newington
London
Warranted.

Its measurements, allowing for the modification of a later point, fit Ward's ideal specification. With its silver mount and ferrule, I imagine that my Grandfather reserved it for special occasions, May Day or the Steeplechases. He would be shy about seeming to give himself airs in the daily traffic of *Novelty* and *Regulator*. But he cherished *Mazeppa's* courtesy, and handed on the keepsake to my father's special care.

## XXII

My Grandfather's Aunt Sarah, the widow of the
Uncle George who had stood bond for his apprenticeship, lived at 18 Walton Street, Oxford, until
her death, supporting a modest dignity in the directory list of Gentry. When she died in 1849, her husband's estate, as we have seen, came into my Grandfather's administration, and this meant increased
substance for John of The Ark's children. George, a
coachman—even though a coachman with silver ferrules to his whip—at Warwick, felt, at the age of
forty-one that he ought to make a move in the world.
Change of any kind in those days was slow, but he
laid his plans. His aunt's will was proved on New
Year's Day 1850; two years later he had taken
his young family to Oxford, and in 1852 was proprietor of The Three Goats, a very ancient hostelry
in that town.

I am indebted to Mr. Henry Minn for particulars
as to its history. It was built in 1588, on the filled-
in-mediæval moat, at what is now the corner of
George Street and Cornmarket. In 1602 one Thomas
Maddox obtained leave to hang out the sign of The

[ 127 ]

Falcon, and in 1621 Robert Wooley, a rich Cord-
wainer, bought the lease, and altered the sign to
Three Goats' Heads, the emblem of his livery, 'he
being a man of competent wealth having a house fit
for an inn with stabling.' There would be thrills if
we could recover the tally of guests at The Falcon
and The Three Goats' Heads of those days; Oxford,
for example, was a very convenient stage on the
road between Stratford and London. Records of the
house disappear until 1804, when Mark and James
Morrell, brewers, bought the lease. It was from them
that my Grandfather took over the house in 1852.
In the following year substantial alterations and
additions were made to the premises, and he changed
the sign to The George. On an opposing corner there
had been from the time of Richard II another George
that in even earlier times had hung out its bush
as Pyper's, or Piper's Inn, but this had long since
disappeared.

By this time the coaching era was in its decline.
In 1838 the Mayor of Oxford had announced that
he 'considered it most unjust and cruel that year
after year the city should be taxed to oppose a bill
so unjustifiable and so uncalled for.' But already
the railways were advancing as inexorably as the
waves upon that earlier Canute. Within a year the
Great Western had puffed its way into Oxford. In

George and Eliza Drinkwater of The George at Oxford.
The George from Broad Street.

1842, Queen Victoria made her first railway journey, from Slough to Paddington. In the town intelligence of Banbury in 1852, the date of my Grandfather's return to Oxford, coaches, that had been so conspicuous a feature of the news, were no longer mentioned as running. Instead, it was announced that the Great Western had trains to town at 8.40, 11.40, 1.40, 4.10, slow at three hours and twenty minutes, fast at two hours and a half. This, it could not be disputed, made even the Flying Machines look silly. There was no substantial saving on fares, but a decisive saving on time. The coaches, in fact, managed to maintain a precarious existence in a remote point-to-point manner until 1870 or so. The *Aurora* even kept some high-road custom from Worcester through Birmingham and down by Oxford to The George and Blue Boar in London as late as 1866. But when my Grandfather went to The Three Goats in 1852, the old drivers who had startled the night with teams of four, and even with teams of six, were mostly disillusioned men in a mad world, many of them with hearts uncommon near to breaking. Those who were young enough to have enterprise left in them could adapt themselves to the new mode, but at the mid-century it was a common thing to find the chimney corners in the taverns occupied of an evening by ageing men who had been masters of an art that was no longer esteemed. The coachmen had been great swells, rotund and impressive figures in the national life; now they were pensioners on friendly upstarts who, in exchange for old stories, would give them the price of a pint.

It may be doubted whether, in terms of adroitness, nerve, and judgment, any finer test of physical character has ever been made in our island story than that imposed on these men who took the coaches over ragged roads in all weathers to scheduled time. Brooklands and the Schneider Cup find competitors in plenty who are willing to face death for a record; but the mechanics of the car and the aeroplane are far less incalculable than the mechanics of a horse. Multiply your horse by four, and three and a bolter at that, and for ten men who can round the earth in a Moth you may search long for one who could have covered the York to London turnpike at eleven miles an hour. The coachmen who sat discarded in the inns of 1850, doubtless in my Grandfather's inn facing the Broad, were the victims of progress; but they knew much, were much, that essentially progress would not better.

It was my Grandfather's luck that when the change came he was not too old to face it. His Oxford house was well situated to take a comfortable share of custom from the town, the University, and the through traffic. He was registered in Corn-market not only as a publican, but as a wine and spirit merchant. Like his brother John of The White Lion at Banbury, he drank but little himself, but he was known among dons and citizens as a judge of what good drink was. If George Drinkwater of The George said that a port or a madeira was worthy of a gentleman's cellar, to the cellar it went. And if a young lord of Christ Church wanted to know about a horse, he knew where to go for his information. In the past days, no coach had come into the city in better style than *Regulator*, and a proctor himself was known to ask his arrest whether Mr. Drink-water's opinion might be consulted on a bay gelding.

My Grandfather kept The George until his death in 1873. At not infrequent intervals, visits were exchanged with his brother John of Banbury. The White Lion in those days was well, almost afflu-ently, kept. Its hostess, dying in 1850, had left the establishment handsomely furnished. For many years her house had been patronised by bagmen visiting the district to offer their wares to the great houses in the neighbourhood. Trade under Victorian auspices was brisk, and at the end of their sessions profits were satisfactory. The residue of their stock was negligible in their accounts, and they were happy to offer it to Mrs. Drinkwater at bargain prices.

And so she accumulated an imposing inventory of plate and china and linen, that made a very pleasing display when guests were entertained. Her husband in widowerhood could receive his brother George with Eliza from Oxford in a manner that was a credit to the best traditions of Banbury hospitality.

# XXIII

THESE brothers, John and George, had inherited and enjoyed the spirit of coaching England. Let us try to recapture it.

The story in perspective is a romantic one, and romance on the road there certainly was. But in the main the coaching life was very hard, and travelling by coach a plaguey uncomfortable business. If you were young, the weather fine, and the road not too bad, a spin on an outside seat through good country was pleasant enough, but the odds against so favourable a conjunction were heavy. There are many records of the discomforts endured by passengers, but the following communication, made by 'C.T.' to *Notes and Queries* in 1856, summarises the complaint, and has, I think, never been reprinted:

'There being some persons who seriously lament the good old times of coaches when they could travel leisurely and securely, see the country and converse with the natives, it may be well to register some of the miseries before they are altogether effaced from the memory. . . .

1st Misery. Although your place has been contingently secured days before, and you have risen with the lark, yet you see the ponderous vehicle arrive full, full, full. And this, not unlikely, more than once.

2. At the end of a stage beholding the four panting, reeking, foaming animals, which have dragged you twelve miles; and the stiff, galled, scraggy relay crawling and limping out of the yard.

3. Being politely requested, at the foot of a tremendous hill, to ease the horses. Mackintoshes, vulcanised India rubber, gutta percha, and gossamer dust-coat, then unknown.

4. An outside passenger resolving to endure no longer "the pelting of the pitiless storm" takes refuge, to your consternation, within with dripping hat, saturated cloak, and soaked umbrella.

5. Set down with a promiscuous party to a meal bearing no resemblance to that of a good hotel, except in the charge; and no time to enjoy it.

6. Closely packed in a box, "cabin'd, crib'd, confin'd, bound in," with five companions morally and physically obnoxious, for two or three comfortless nights and days.

7. During a halt overhearing the coarse language of the ostlers and tipplers at the roadside pothouse; and besieged by beggars exposing their mutilations.

8. Roused from your nocturnal slumber by the horn or bugle, the testing and cracking of whip, turnpike gates, a search for parcels under your seat, and solicitous drivers.

9. Discovering at a divergent point in your jour-

ney that the "Tally Ho" runs only every other day or so, or has finally stopped.

10. Clambering from the wheel by various iron projections to your elevated seat.

11. After threading the narrowest streets of an ancient town, entering the inn-yard by a low gateway, at the imminent risk of decapitation.

12. Seeing the baggage piled 'Olympus high,' so as to occasion an alarming oscillation.

13. Having the reins and whip placed in your unpracticed hands while coachee indulges in a glass and a chat.

14. Dangling at the end of a seat overcome with drowsiness.

15. Exposed to piercing draughts, owing to a refractory glass; or, *vice versa*, being in a minority, you are compelled, for the sake of ventilation, to thrust your umbrella accidentally through a pane.

16. At various seasons, suffocated with dust, and broiled by a powerful sun; or cowering under an umbrella in a drenching rain—or petrified with cold —or torn by fierce winds—or struggling through snow—or wending your way through perilous floods.

17. Perceiving that a young squire is receiving an initiatory practical lesson in the art of driving, or that a jibbing horse, or a race with an opposition, is endangering your existence.

18. Losing the enjoyment or employment of much precious time not only on the road, but also from consequent fatigue.

19. Interrupted before the termination of your

hurried meal by your two rough-coated, big-buttoned, many-caped friends, the coachman and guard, who hope you will remember them. Although the gratuity has been repeatedly calculated in anticipation, you fail in making the mutual remembrancer agreeable.'

Blameless as this account may be of exaggeration, the conditions of coaching travel as known by 'C. T.' were a vast improvement on those of a yet earlier time. In 1784, John Palmer, the son and London agent of the proprietor of two Bath theatres, succeeded in interesting William Pitt the younger in his scheme for making the stage-coaches carriers for His Majesty's Mail, which had hitherto been conveyed by post-boys of incredible tardiness. The experiment was an immediate and spectacular success. On the evening of August 2nd, two coaches set out from the extremities of the London and Bristol road, watched with great interest by the public and ill-concealed jealousy by the Post Office authorities. On Tuesday morning they reached Bristol and London respectively well in advance of Palmer's timetable, which itself had been considered irresponsibly sanguine. Within a week the journey was being made regularly in less than thirteen hours. The Post Office revenue rose rapidly, and in 1786 Palmer was appointed Controller. From that date there was, under his influence, continuous improvement in the construction, comfort, and efficiency of the coaches. Bone-shaking was not abolished, but it was alleviated, and the risk of being bogged or even drowned in mud gradually disappeared. Seating accommodation of five feet six inches for four people was a poor, if parliamentary, allowance, but by 1800 'spanking' was no longer a euphemism for the coaches that enjoyed the custom of the Royal Mails, and their less fortunate rivals could survive only by offering the public a highly competitive service. The cost, as well as the inconvenience of travelling gradually decreased. In 1731 the fare on the Birmingham stage to London was a guinea. Ninety years later, on the *Balloon*, the first coach that Bill Bayzand could remember running out of Oxford for town, driven by Bobart, 'the Classical Coachman,' a graduate of the University, the fares were twenty-five shillings for an inside seat, eighteen shillings outside. By 1840, these had been reduced to twelve shillings and eight. The first forty or fifty years of the new century, when the Drinkwaters were on the road, were the zenith of the coaching business, and at no centre was the business more robustly active than in Oxford.

# XXIV

Of this activity a remarkably interesting record has been preserved. In 1884, the Bodleian Library bought from Mr. William Bayzand, then janitor at the Radcliffe Camera, the manuscript of notes that he had made on 'Coaching In and Out of Oxford from 1820 to 1840.' This was none other than the Bill Bayzand who in his time had been a celebrated guard on the London-Hereford *Mazeppa*. The manuscript was subsequently printed in the Transactions of the Oxford Historical Society.

Bayzand could recall the days when coming and going the Oxford inns saw seventy-three coaches daily—he thought there were more, but he could speak for those. A great many of them were Oxford built, by William Shackleford, my Grandfather's master, and others. The standard bulk of these was eighteen hundredweight, and they were designed to 'carry the heaviest load you could put on without the slightest rocking or rolling.' What the load could be, Bayzand describes:

'Four [passengers] inside and twelve out; coachman, fifteen stone, myself, eleven; with as much luggage as I could stack on the roof and as we were allowed to carry by Act of Parliament, securely made fast with four wide, leather straps, covered and made waterproof with tarpaulin; the front and hind boots full, and covered with waterproof; with cradle slung on the hind axle-tree, full of fish, and on every available part of the coach, packages of all kinds hanging on the lamp-irons, and ladies' band-boxes, with light articles, strapped on the seat-irons.'

Altogether, 'the four horses had behind them something like two tons and a half.'

Bayzand draws a vivid picture of an Oxford scene in which for many years he was himself one of the liveliest figures. He takes us round the city at an early morning hour, halting first outside The Angel in the High, where ten coaches are already lined up along the street; porters, ostlers and guards busy with a rattle of interjections as they make a final inspection of traces, chains, harness, luggage. Already the passengers are in their seats, the boys at the leaders' heads, and the coachmen up on their boxes, gently stroking the wheelers with their whips, and taking large turnip watches from ample frontages for frequent consultation. And then the signal is heard, Queen's clock striking eight. The boys stand back, the guards swing into their places, the yard servants cry 'right away,' and the departure is led by the Cambridge post, four bays, heading for Magdalen bridge on its eighty-two mile journey. Close behind follow *The Alert*, driven by Black Will, with four chestnuts, for London, and *Hero*, with four blacks, for Brighton. Up to Carfax, for the south, go 'old Mr. John Bayzand with his four long-tailed blacks' for Southampton; for the west, the Bath and Bristol post with a pair of grays, and *The Isis* with a pair of blacks for Cheltenham; and for the north, *Rising Sun*, driven by John Bamshaw, known as Civil John, also with a pair of blacks, for Northampton; the *Day* for Birmingham, with four browns, and, with his four browns also, George Drinkwater up on *Regulator* for Warwick. An hour later, the tenth coach leaves alone, the *Light Oxford* with four bays for London.

This was the beginning of the coaching day, and the activity went on till nightfall. At a little before nine o'clock the *Blenheim*, famous for its four dapple-grays, was standing outside The Star, waiting for the branch from Chipping Norton before starting for The Blue Boar in Holborn. At ten o'clock *Defiance* left The Mitre with four grays for London, and the Reading post an hour later. At eleven, too, *The Age* left The Vine for Town with a mixed team, driven by the brothers George and Joseph Tollit, who challenged opposition with the slogan 'Economy without Monopoly.' At the same

hour *The Royal William* left The Golden Cross
in Cornmarket, also for London, and for years there
was keen rivalry between its four browns driven by
William and Richard Snowden, and the mixed team
of the Tollits, both families being driver-proprietors. One May Day a formal trial of speed from
London was made, Joseph Tollit up on *The Age*,
William Snowden on *The Royal William*. The
coaches kept sight of each other throughout the journey, and both were timed into Oxford at three hours
and twenty minutes for the fifty-four miles.

The morning was well advanced before the last
departure was out, and already the arrivals had
begun to come in. These, says Bayzand, 'caused the
greatest pitch of excitement.' At eleven o'clock, as
*The Age* and *The Royal William* left The Vine and
The Golden Cross, *Magnet* drew up at The Star in
Cornmarket from Cheltenham, its opposition, the
*Berkeley Hunt*, making all way to be no later at
The Angel from the same stage. Both were crack
coaches, doing 'the ninety-seven miles, including all
stoppages, in nine hours.' At the same hour John
Drinkwater's *Novelty* came in to The Mitre from
Banbury, to leave again at half-past five. At half-
past twelve *Retaliator* was in from Gloucester, at
one o'clock *Sovereign* from Worcester and *Triumph*
from Birmingham, running from The Hen and

Chickens in New Street, to be followed an hour later by *Tantivy* from the same town. At half-past two *Mazeppa* from Hereford set down Bill Bayzand himself with his load at The Roebuck.

News can never have had the same tang since the days when it was taken through the town from the inn-yards by word of mouth. The incoming coaches were the chief intelligencers of the time, and within a few minutes of their arrival there was an eager buzz of gossip drifting away to the taverns and by-ways. At moments of national excitement, the coaches were waylaid by a continuous ambush of inquiry on the roads; a ploughman would shout his question over the hedge, well-pleased with a word of answer, and the population of hamlets too inconspicuous for official notice would mob the guard's seat at a run, a mile into the open country. Epochal events, Trafalgar or Waterloo, would send the coaches out of London garlanded with oak-leaves, and the fortunate messengers could make what levies they liked on a transported people. Bayzand, who by some means was able to secure copies of *The Times* at six o'clock in London before he made his morning start on *Mazeppa*, tells how he was besieged by bidders along the western road on the day when it was known that the Reform Bill of 1832 had become law. Four browns or four bays, the successive stages were vocal with 'Has the Bill passed?' At Shottenham, a gentleman gave a sovereign for a copy of the paper; at Ross the price had risen to two sovereigns; and on arrival at Hereford, the guard was carried shoulder-high to Mr. Bosley's inn, where the precious journal changed hands for a five-pound note on the Hereford Old Bank, and having been read aloud to a cheering company, was 'framed, glazed and hung up in the Club Room for many years.'

During the Oxford evenings the short-distance returns went out, *Novelty* to Banbury, the Witney stage from The Three Cups, and the like. And even through the night the yards were never deserted. At nine o'clock *Champion* was in from Hereford, on the way to London, or at eleven down from Town going west. '*Champion* was noted for carrying extremely heavy loads, particularly in the salmon season, from the River Wye.' At eleven *The Telegraph* arrived from Worcester. At midnight the ostlers of The Star were ready with a fresh team for *Paul Pry*, bound to London from Aberystwith, at one o'clock in the morning *Union* made its stage at The Golden Cross from Birmingham, and at three the *Prince of Wales* from the same town at The Angel. On every route cross-country connections were made at frequent intervals. And then there

[ 143 ]

were the Royal Mails, in and out of the city through the small hours, connecting London with the Midlands, the West, the Severn valley, and Wales. If any passenger were so bold as to take the road at night on foot, he could hardly walk a mile out of Oxford between sunset and dawn without encountering the blaze of lamps and the pounding of hooves.

It must be remembered that most of these units passed through the town in duplicate every twenty-four hours, the usual service of any stage being made in both directions daily. In November 1828, members of the public were informed that *The Guide* would leave The Angel at half-past seven in the morning, reach London at one-thirty noon, take the return road at two, and be again in Oxford at eight. Also, there were the auxiliary and private vehicles. Richard Costar, the principal proprietor in the town, advertised from his office in the High that he was prepared to provide a post-coach for London at any unscheduled time 'to accomodate a party.'

Bayzand, with the relish of a connoisseur, adds to his annals of the public stages a pretty account of the gentry on the road. 'It was,' he says, 'a pleasure to see his lordship, the Earl of Abingdon, bring his four chestnuts up to The Star so readily, and look, as he always did, so satisfied.' Sir Henry

[ 144 ]

Peyton, of Swifts House, had a yellow coach with four grays, handled them himself, and was 'a first-class performer in every respect.' Lord Dillon, of Ditchley Park, drove four bays, while the Duke of Marlborough, with a like team, turned out with postillions and outriders, 'looking like royalty.' Edward Quick, Esq., of New College, had four chestnuts, and wore 'a drab driving-coat built by Mrs. Jones, St. Clement's.' She was a noted tailoress for box-coats [note: the origin of box-cloth]; price from twelve to sixteen guineas, with as many capes. Aston Smith, also Esq.,—whom Bayzand calls Haston—drove four grays, and had a fancy for giving lifts to 'any poor man or woman on business to Oxford.' He was never known to drive into the city with an empty coach.

The Provost of Worcester drove a pair of browns, as did the Warden of Merton and the Bishop of Oxford, while the President of St. John's favoured chestnuts. Lord Valentia, from Bletchington, was a notable figure on the box with four roans, 'elbows close to his side, hands down, shoulders well back, his head erect, his eyes well in front.' Strawberry roans they were, 'good, even workers, pace and temper united.' I myself remember an impressive Lord Valentia, when he hunted Bicester hounds, with moustaches only less remarkable than those sported

by his contemporary, Mr. Hermon Hodge, now Lord
Wyfold. Then there were the Hon. Colonel Parker
of Sherbourne Castle, with four bays, and Slater
Harrison, Esq., with four grays, both of them masters in a degree that provoked the admiration of a
professional so tested as the *Mazeppa* guard.

Add to the scene, on winter mornings, forty
hunters and hacks waiting in Turl Street, their
riders, from Lincoln, Exeter and Jesus, dressed in
pink; as many again at Canterbury Gate from
Oriel and Merton. And 'if you walked a little distance on the road, you would see a dozen or more
tandems ready to take gentlemen on to cover.'

## XXV

Such was the daily circumstance in which my people took their part. Class-distinction was sharp enough in those days, but a man who could take a team of four securely round the Oxford corners, whether 'scraping' or 'sweeping,' was treated with respect in any company. Dressed, as Leigh Hunt tells us, in 'a frock-coat, with mother-o'-pearl buttons, a striped yellow waistcoat, and a flower in his mouth,' the coachman of *Regulator* or *Novelty* might touch his beaver to My Lord Valentia, but My Lord was willing to acknowledge that there was a peerage other than that defined by Westminster.

Money, said Falstaff, is a good soldier, and will on. But a better soldier yet is skill. It was at one time my good fortune to play cricket in an eleven with Dick Lilley, the greatest keeper, to my mind, who ever stood behind the wicket for England. To stand up to Tom Richardson at his fastest was a folly only justified by Lilley's results. It always seemed to me a very odd thing that a man who for years had been on equal terms with nobs of the aristocracy should have learnt so little from their superficial manners. He was, for example, always uncertain as to the relative functions of a knife and a fork at table. In more ponderable matters he was a gentleman right enough. I used to go in first with him; also I used to get out first. And when he in turn came back to the pavilion, he would seek me out to say, 'that ball would have beat me all over.' That is being a gentleman. It was not only his superlative cricket, but also his charming conduct in this kind, that made him an intimate of all the M.C.C. silver spoons. A skilled boor could never have come by his personal prestige. Nevertheless, being so notably not a boor, it was the skill that was the good soldier and, despite table inaccuracies, would on. Class-considerations were lost in that inspiring spectacle as Dick stood up to Tom with Victor Trumper's bat between them.

As it happens, John and George Drinkwater, respectively of The White Lion and The George or Three Goats, were well advised in the matter of prongs and green peas. But they had no blue blood in their veins; they came of stock that had mostly drawn an agricultural labourer's wages in Tackley when it had escaped the workhouse. And yet they were esteemed by the Quality; not with condescension, but with recognition of skill. They could handle the ribbons with any man on the road, and that, with a staunch dignity of character, was enough.

Their calling was rich in racy incident. Thomas Hardy in his diary tells of a man in Sturminster who was so excited when a coach was put on the road from Poole to Bristol, that on the morning of its first journey 'he got up early, swept the whole street, and sprinkled sand for the vehicle and horses to pass over.' That was in 1770 or so, but although half a century had made the coaches familiar objects to everyone, it had not made them commonplace. In every town they had become part of the daily routine, and yet they had not suffered, rather had they matured, in style and romance. The discomforts and hardships of the road, so feelingly chronicled by 'C. T.,' were notorious. Let Bill Bayzand, his vocation ruined by the railways, recall another picture:

'All the coach roads are wonderfully improved throughout England. The travelling of all coaches was great, compassing their ten to twelve miles per hour. Coaches were exceedingly comfortable, and at all times carried life and jollity with them; the fares, generally speaking, moderate; coachman and guards intelligent, pleasant, and, as a general rule, civil, obliging, and always well-dressed. The teams were made up with short-legged, quick-stepping cattle, well matched for pace, working exceedingly well together. It was pleasing to sit behind them and see them so exquisitely handled. The change

of horses was like magic; sometimes, if no interfer-
ence from a passenger with coachman, guard or
horse-keeper, in less than a minute; the guard's words
"Right! we'll pull up at the top of the hill to wash
their mouths out; we shall have time to take a glass"
—a blast from the horn to remind the good-tem-
pered-looking, smiling barmaid to be in readiness for
the arrival of the coach—refreshed with a foaming
tankard of real, sparkling, home-brewed beer, made
from real malt and hops, the horn sounded to "take
your seats"; on we go through a delightful country,
the perfume from the fresh cut grass, or from a bean,
pea, or clover field, smelling far more sweet than
the rancid oil, grease, and smothered in smoke and
steam on a railway trip.'

Not often, it may be conceded to 'C. T.' was it
all as idyllic as that, but, even so, for the men who
lived by the road, its humours and satisfactions—
we might say, its rewards and fairies—made its
asperities not very difficult to bear. If, with the
hazards of weather and mishap, every day was an
ordeal, it was also an adventure, and often a very
agreeable one. Even driver-proprietors like the
Drinkwaters made no fortunes; a decent competence
was all they could hope for, and, indeed, usually all
that they desired. But they loved their coaches, and
as one by one these were drawn into the yards for
the last time, obsolete and their occupation gone,

some irrecoverable zest had gone, too, from their masters' lives.

Many of the coachmen at the end could look back on remarkable records. Old John Bayzand, when he first drove between Oxford and Southampton, did the journey in twelve hours; thirty-six years later he was still on the same road, and his allowance was seven. He stepped down from the box for the last time, grown from a young to an old man in the service, without a single accident against his account.

Bayzand the younger, confirmed as he was to the road, was too shrewd to disregard facts. 'Bayzand,' the sceptics would say to him, 'if your head never aches till the railways come, it will be a long time.' But he determined to see for himself. He took the coach to Manchester, and thence went by rail second class to Liverpool. Covering the thirty-four miles in an hour and five minutes, he knew that the coaches were doomed.

## XXVI

My Grandfather knew this life in its heyday and in its decline, was bred to its manners, its rigours, its idiom. Like his brother John, he was a genial, friendly man, and as hardy. He was a good friend, but not one with whom to take liberties. He had very kind eyes. He was fastidious about his hands, and liked a buttonhole of cornflowers, widely worn as the coaching favour.

He lived temperately, but with a liberal zest for enjoyment and fun. His well-regulated mind took a keen pleasure in such pastimes and diversions as came within his means, and opportunity was not scant. He gave himself no airs, and tolerated none in others. He liked the story told by Bill Bayzand of William Holland, the well-to-do proprietor of The Golden Cross. Paying a visit in Hampshire he lost his way, and, accosting a country lad, enquired in a patronising voice, 'Jack, which is the way to Stockbridge?' ' 'Ow ded thee know my name were Jack?' 'Oh, I guessed it.' 'Then thee guess thy road to Stockbridge.'

May festival was show day for the coaches. In

George Drinkwater. (The author's grandfather.)

London all the Mails met in St. Paul's Churchyard, shining in new paint and harness, their teams groomed to a glorious sheen, and decked out in ribbons and rosettes. A procession was formed, led by Bristol, the oldest Mail on the road, and proceeded to the General Post Office, in St. Martin's-le-Grand, where the coachmen and guards were given new liveries, red coats, gilt buttons, dark-blue waistcoats, black hats trimmed with gold lace with a black rosette. Here the Postmaster General had provided a lavish spread with good wine. And then, Bristol still leading, through the streets of London to St. James's, where the procession lined up before the Palace, and coachmen and guards, brightly decorated with nosegays, stood up in their seats to salute the Sovereign.

The coaches throughout the country emulated the example of the Royal Mails, and on May Day at Oxford the streets and inn-yards saw the stages in a carnival of spring flowers and fancies. Among them, and as debonair as any, were *Novelty* and *Regulator*, and as they drove in and out of Banbury, there, too, might be met John's *Rival* and *Original Sovereign*, and in later years *The Union Railway*, bright in new colour and varnish, rosetted like the rest, and knotted with cowslips and bluebells from The White Lion meadows.

My Grandfather, even with the depletion of coaching revenue and custom, managed to support the fortunes of The George at Oxford in creditable style. He articled his eldest son to an architect; and was able to provide the money necessary to supplement the scholarship—or postmastership as it is known—won by my Father from Magdalen College School to Merton. My Uncle Harry, born in 1844, could remember his father while he still drove stage. His frequent requests as a boy to be allowed to sit beside the box-seat on a journey, were met with a promise that he should do so when he was old enough to smoke a cigar. The terms of this undertaking seemed ambiguous, and induced him to make a premature effort to fulfil the condition laid down, with melancholy consequences.

With my Father at Magdalen School was Charles Brown, whose sister he was to marry. The families were long acquainted, and I cannot but suppose that John Beck Brown might sometimes leave his fire-irons and coulters and have a friendly half-hour with George Drinkwater, his neighbour a few doors north up the Cornmarket. When my Father was born, in 1852, it was still the fashion to christen babies after the Prince of Wales, and I suspect that his Albert Edwin was due to the slip of a sponsor's tongue.

I have already told what I know of his athletic feats at school and the 'Varsity. I have a medal, a very solid affair in silver handsomely embossed with the Magdalen lilies, inscribed round the rim 'Mathematics 1871. A. E. Drinkwater.' Although he disappointed his tutors by taking a third instead of a first in his final Schools, he went down with a scholastic reputation that had not been altogether forfeited by his failure.

He rode, perfunctorily, but the family instinct for horses was more generously inherited by his brother Harry, eight years his elder, who could drive tandem, and even that rare and very ticklish team, unicorn. My Father, who in later years was of a robust, rather stockish build, was spare and pale as a young man, for all his hundred in ten and a fifth. Harry from the first had the square jaw of their father, though later, oddly enough, my Father developed this too. A photograph, taken about 1870, shows the three of them in the season's suitings, all wearing regulation alberts, my Uncle Harry affecting braid to his coat and what appears to be a sprig of may in his buttonhole.

Three years later my Grandfather died. His will, of which he appointed his wife Eliza sole executrix, was drawn on August 3rd, 1872, he died on February 1st following, and it was proved on the 25th, his estate being sworn at 'under Two Thousand Pounds.' Of this sum, five hundred and sixty-eight pounds was represented by a life policy in the Atlas Assurance Company.

On his death, his children induced their mother to leave The George; I fancy that the professional ambitions of the brothers made them think it a good opportunity to drop out of the hotel business, since my Grandmother, a considerate but rather formidable old lady, was perfectly capable of running The George or any other establishment that she might have chosen to give her mind to. She moved for a time to a private residence in Oxford, and then to Leamington. When she died, in 1893, she left four hundred and fifty-two pounds, two shillings and tenpence, to be divided in equal parts between her four children, and to be administered by her sons Harry George Walter and Albert Edwin.

# XXVII

My father was elected to his Merton Postmastership in 1870. Having taken his third after a second in Moderations, he did a little coaching in Oxford for a time, and in 1876 was appointed to the second mastership of St. Andrew's College, at Chardstock in Dorset. In 1879 he became head master of the Coburn Foundation School at Bow, in the east of London. His application for the former post was supported by William Esson, a Fellow of the Royal Society, who had been his tutor at Oxford, thus: 'He obtained a second class in Moderations at a time when the standard had been suddenly raised, and I feel sure that in an ordinary year he would have obtained a first. In the final schools he did not do himself justice; the quality of his work with me was much higher than was represented by the class he obtained.' His heart, however, was not really in all this. A warning note is sounded by another tutor: 'He is not only a very fair all-round mathematician with special interest in and very thorough knowledge of such less artificial Mathematics (Geometry for instance), as a Schoolmaster has mainly to deal with, but has also strong literary and artistic tastes and interests that give him qualifications which no specialist can have.' Our more enlightened ideas of education might accept that as a satisfactory testimonial, but in 1879, when it was written, it must have been disturbing in some quarters what with its talk about a fair Mathematician and artistic tastes, and the defects of specialism. It was all very well for Mandell Creighton, then Vicar of Chathill and afterwards Bishop of London, who had been my father's Dean at Merton, to write that while he had had nothing to do with his teaching, and must 'therefore leave others to testify to his ability,' he could 'speak very highly of his character and conduct.' The fact was that, while my Father was an efficient master and by common consent an excellent influence in the schools at which he worked, academic occupation was for him never attractive enough to encourage the full exercise of his talents.

On moving to Coburn, he took a house at Leytonstone, which he named 'Dorset Villa' in memory of Chardstock. It stood in what was then the open country of Fairlop Road, was re-named 'Albany House' in 1888, and became just No. 105 in 1894. In 1882 my Father appears in Kelly's Directory as Albert Edward Drinkwood, of Leytonstone, and in that year, on the first of June, I was born. The Registrar of Births was more accurate than Kelly.

In 1884 my Father moved from Leytonstone to 12 Clapton Square. It was there that the German-Band wolf looked in at my window. I remember nothing else of the house, the first home that I can recall being 1 Ladbrooke Crescent, Notting Hill, which I left for Oxford when I was nine.

In 1886 my Father prepared a little leaflet of testimonials, apparently in support of some further scholastic ambition. But by that time the call of the theatre had finally asserted itself, and shortly afterwards he secured his first professional engagement on the stage—an unfamiliar stage for the Drinkwaters—with Hermann Vezin. The adventure was viewed by my Mother with some anxiety, if not distress. She was ill at ease in the strange new society of players who began to frequent the house. She had no enthusiasm for the theatre. Also, she was convinced that it was a dangerously precarious calling, and in this at least she was right. From the day he left schoolmastering, my Father was always profoundly happy in his work, but for many years it brought him no material success, and even when in later days he had found some security, he suffered to the end from a sense that early hopes had not been realised.

His career would afford suitable material for a modern psychological novel. I cannot say how good an actor he was. Naturally I thought him excellent, and he was reasonably fortunate in his engagements with men like Edward Terry, John Hare, and Charles Wyndham. But, although he had discarded formal scholarship, he remained something of a scholar. He even conducted a correspondence in Greek with his friend, Jack Witcher, actuary of the Sun Life Office, who gave me Hans Andersen's *Fairy Tales* on my eighth birthday. In the middle 'eighties of last century the intellectual state of the English theatre was not encouraging to a man whose mind had some background. There were the travelling stock companies, playing classics almost entirely in terms of melodrama, and my Father found some congenial employment with these, touring with Harbury-Matthews and Mrs. Bandmann-Palmer, the lady who created a sensation by playing Hamlet, and over five hundred times. But he was ambitious also to help in the foundation of an intelligent contemporary drama, and, in this, light and leading were far to seek.

He wanted to write plays, and to become his own manager. Robertson's *Caste*, which had been produced in 1867, was still the standard of modern achievement. But, admirable as it was, it had little to say to a new generation that was just beginning to demand more athletic thought and greater distinction of style in the theatre. When the reformation came, for in the light of subsequent events it can hardly be said to have been less than that, it came sharply divided against itself. Henry Arthur Jones was born in 1851. He made a popular success with *The Silver King* in 1882, but it was not until the 'nineties that he established himself as a leader of the new movement. Similarly, Arthur Wing Pinero, born in 1855, although he had produced his first playet in 1876, was known in the middle 'eighties as a writer of such diverting farces as *Dandy Dick* and *The Magistrate*, and not until the 'nineties as the dramatist of the remarkable series of plays that provoked excited discussion by their problematic nature, and general admiration by their mastery of the stage. But just at the time when these men were bringing new scope and impetus to the theatre, another fresh intelligence was attacking their methods and their ideas with irrepressible vigour. In 1892, Bernard Shaw, who was born in 1856, became associated with the Independent Theatre, sponsored by J. T. Grein. Of this event he afterwards wrote:

'I turned my hand to playwriting when a great deal of talk about "The New Drama," followed by the actual establishment of a "New" Theatre, threatened to end in the humiliating discovery that the New Drama, in England at all events, was a figment of the revolutionary imagination. This was not to be endured. I had rashly taken up the case, and, rather than let it collapse, I manufactured the evidence.'

The 'evidence' began with *Mrs. Warren's Profession* which was produced by Grein's theatre in 1892 and followed by Miss Horniman's production of *Arms and the Man* at the old Avenue in 1894. Simultaneously, the assault on the Jones-Pinero supremacy was delivered. The merits of that controversy are of no present concern, but the indecisive impact made by Shaw's first plays was strongly reinforced by his critical campaign from 1895-1898 in *The Saturday Review* against current modes. The 'evidence,' which has gone on being 'manufactured' so vigorously since, speaks for itself, but the fact remains that his magnificent tirades of now nearly forty years ago were directed against men who were as genuinely reformers of the theatre as himself.

## XXVIII

IT was into this dramatic vortex that my Father, at
the age of thirty-four, strayed from the class-rooms
of Chardstock and Bow. And his misfortune was that
he was one of the few people who at the time recognised that there was any vortex at all. Had he been
a youngster with an intelligence quick enough to perceive the Shavian direction from the first, or if, on
the other hand, he had merely been aware of the
Pineroic influence, his gifts might have had a better
chance. But he began too late. The intelligence was
quick enough, but he was not a youngster, and he was
involved in the difficulty of being sensitive to the
merits of both parties. The result was that, not having great originating power, he never formed any
clear purpose in his own dramatic writing. I often
heard him say that he regarded Pinero as the greatest
dramatist of the age; but also he was, in a strictly
practical sense, one of the first gospellers of Shaw in
the country.

So that my Father's playwriting never brought
him the recognition for which he always hoped. In
1885 he published a book of *Plays and Poems*,

which reached a second edition in the following year. The plays were in verse, and the best scene in them is a brief excursion in yokel humour taken from Dorset models. In after years he scored an occasional success, particularly with his one-act plays, and as late as 1922, when he was seventy, he published *The Pipe of Peace*, an essay in sociological drama full of high purpose and fine temper. But the style, in all its implications, had never become quite assured. The most effective thing that he ever did as a dramatist was to work over *The Farmer's Wife*, a service always acknowledged by Eden Phillpotts in the most generous manner. But he did not live to enjoy the remarkable success of that play.

Admiring Pinero in the revolutionary centre, he was, as I have said, an immediate admirer also of Shaw on the left. *Arms and The Man*, when it was produced at the Avenue in 1884, ran for ten weeks, and my Father applied at once for provincial rights. I asked Mr. Shaw what he could recall of the circumstances, and he writes, January 15, 1931:

'. . . Your father, fired by a mad ambition to play the part of Bluntschli, insisted on taking the piece on tour in spite of my attempts to dissuade him. Kremlin played Petkoff and produced the play. He began his duties in the manner of a drill sergeant, with the immediate result that the actor engaged to

*Top*—Gerald Lawrence as *Sergius*, Lilian M. Revell as *Louka*, A. E. Drinkwater as *Bluntschli* in Bernard Shaw's *Arms and the Man*, 1895. *Bottom*—A. E. Drinkwater as *Bluntschli*.

play Nicola told him off in the most trenchant Billingsgate and shook the dust off his feet as he retired. I had to explain to Kremlin—with an eye to your father—that actors were now university men and wouldn't stand that sort of thing.

The tour was not a financial success, and was soon deep enough in my debt to enable me to extricate your father by offering to cry off my fees if he would cry off the tour, which he accordingly did. This established the cordial relations which always subsisted between us. I saw a good deal of him later on when he managed for Lillah McCarthy at the Kingsway.'

My Father took out the tour, which started on September 8, 1894, in conjunction with Lilian M. Revell, whom he married after my Mother's death. She played the part of Louka. That it was 'not a financial success' is abundantly shown by figures with which also Mr. Shaw has been good enough to supply me. Twice in thirty weeks the gross for the week reached three figures: £109 11s. 7d. at Sheerness and Southend; and £108 3s. at Manchester. At Buxton they did £15 on the week, at Brighton £17, and at Yarmouth £22. Lowestoft turned £80, and £70 was reached at Belfast, Liverpool, Southport, Hastings and Stratford. The average gross weekly takings over the thirty weeks was £51. The date at South Shields, which returned £55 6s. 6d, was augmented by the receipts for a special matinée for which I have a ticket before me, written in manuscript:

*Theatre Royal*
*South Shields*
*"Candida"*
*Special Matinée Saturday*
*March 30, 1895*
*Private Box—One Guinea*

This was the copyright performance of the play, which was subsequently produced on tour by Janet Achurch and Charrington, before its London performance by the Stage Society in 1900. At South Shields my Father played Majoribanks.

A few further notes on my Father will take me beyond the design of this part of my story, which is to close with my leaving school in 1897. From my childhood, I remember his house being stored in every available space with logs and beams of old oak. Once, I believe, he purchased the entire timber of a sixteenth-century cottage that was being demolished. He was a cabinet-maker and wood-carver of quite remarkable accomplishment, and many pieces of his craftsmanship bear witness to a mastery that would not shame a Jacobean. I regarded with less enthusiasm his passion for bicycling. I used in my youth to accompany him on terrifying journeys. A friend had

# Theatre Royal, South Shields.

Sole Lessee and Manageress ... ... ... ... Mrs. L. M. Snowdon.
Acting Manager ... ... ... ... ... ... Mr. Fred Coulson.

### Special Matinee, March 30th, 1895,

By the Members of the "ARMS AND THE MAN" Company, under the direction of
Mr. A. E. Drinkwater.

At 11-30 a.m., for the First Time on any Stage, will be performed

# CANDIDA

A Domestic Play in Three Acts, by

## BERNARD SHAW.

This will be the sole performance of Mr. Shaw's new play in England, prior to its
production at the Fifth Avenue Theatre, New York, by

### MR. RICHARD MANSFIELD.

The play will be introduced to the English Public in South Shields at the Author's
special request by the "ARMS AND THE MAN" Company.

The Characters will be created by the following Members of the Company.

| | |
|---|---|
| Eugene Marjoribanks ... ... ... ... | ... Mr. A. E. Drinkwater. |
| The Rev. James Mavor Morell ... ... ... | ... Mr. George Young. |
| Burgess ... ... ... ... ... ... | ... Mr. F. Crealin. |
| Lexy Mill ... ... ... ... ... | ... Mr. J. Daniels. |
| Proserpine Garnett ... ... ... ... | ... Miss Ethel Verne. |

AND

Candida ... ... ... ... ... ... ... Miss Lilian M. Revell.

Scene.—Study and Sitting Room in St. Dominic's Parsonage, Victoria Park,
East London.

| Period. ... ... ... ... ... | The Present. |
|---|---|
| Act I. ... ... ... ... ... | Morning. |
| Act II. ... ... ... ... ... | Afternoon. |
| Act III. ... ... ... ... ... | Evening. |

Price of Admission to all parts of the House, One Guinea.

NO FEES.

Doors open at 11-20.

Acting Manager ... ... ... ... ... ... Mr. Louis Weighton.

Daybill and Ticket for the first (copyright) performance
of Bernard Shaw's *Candida*, at South Shields, 1895.

given him a very superior Lea and Francis machine, but I was less fortunate in my mount. Its most memorable feature was a tyre of which the inner tube was a two ended affair, like a snake. This was, with great difficulty, inserted already inflated into a six-inch slit in the outer cover, which was then cemented on to the rim. A puncture was, therefore, attended by an operation that reduced one to despair. And there would usually be a puncture or two on my expeditions with him. He would leave me to it, saying he would ride slowly on. Then would follow, after a long interval, an exasperated chase. Once, on a seventy-nine mile ride from Folkestone to London, after several such delays, my lamp-wick gave out in the evening. He improvised a new one from a canvas tie which he was wearing. Then his own gave out. He took a chance and rode close behind me. In Westbourne Grove at midnight my lamp caught fire. He told me to ride on, which I did, a flaming beacon in front of his darkness. A startled constable called upon the apparition to stop, and still I was bidden to ride on. We passed the law at twelve miles an hour, and disappeared towards the fastnesses of Notting Hill.

## XXIX

His early experience of theatrical lodgings had taught him all the refinements of domestic economy. He kept a good table, but it was supplied by his own expert knowledge of the cheapest markets for the best fare in every part of London. So, too, with his dress. He was very careful of his appearance, and paid less for a suit of clothes or a pair of boots than seemed possible. He took an epicurean pride in a delicious orange liqueur that he made himself in large quantities. As a special mark of favour he would give a bottle to a friend.

His early days in Oxfordshire had imbued him with a lasting love of the countryside. He had, I think, no exact ornithological knowledge, but he would often ride out to Richmond Park to sit under some secluded tree to watch the birds. I well remember his eagerness when a green woodpecker once alighted on a bough almost within hand-reach. Sometimes he went fishing with me, but his practice had been with a float in the Oxfordshire water-meadows, and he never took easily to a dry fly. In fact, he was always uncertain—genuinely uncertain—as to the ethics of up and down stream. Standing on the town bridge at Fairford and dangling a mayfly on the current along the garage wall, he was shocked to hear a contemplative inhabitant exclaim 'Dam' old poacher!'

From the time I went to school I saw very little of him until I had grown up; in later years we were on terms of close intimacy again. His theatrical movements made it not always convenient for me to be with him even during my school holidays. When I was, I found some difficulty in adjusting my small mind from its Oxford environment to his more liberal outlook. My Grandfather Brown, as I have shown, was an easy-going man, but in matters of convention he was mostly content to take the line of least resistance. It was, for example, perplexing to me to be told casually by my Father, as we were walking up one Sunday to spend the evening with old Mr. Revell, that they would play whist. It merely had never occurred to me that it was not wicked to play cards on Sunday. Stranger still, Mr. Revell himself struck me as much the most impressive person I had ever seen, with a beautiful head and great authority of manner. If he played cards on Sunday, then it must be all right. He had been a clergyman, but had left the church on account of intellectual scruples which he explained in a book of challenging essays, *Ethical Forecasts*. He had some asthmatic trouble, and I remember the room in which we sat as being hermetically sealed and highly heated by a gas-fire. It was Christmas time, and he gave me a copy of *Trilby*, saying that it was a book with 'a lovely atmosphere.' I did not know what that meant, but I liked the book.

He told me that he had known Browning, but that did not mean anything to me either. I remember that it was at this time that I learnt from my Father that Swinburne, who was a poet, was still alive. I had taken it for granted that all poets were dead, and although I had actually heard the name of Swinburne and that he was a poet, I thought he was a friend of Shakespeare. On the same holiday, my Father told me that he had no belief in the religion taught in the churches, but that he felt great respect for the convictions of those who had. He had, he said, an equal impatience with those people who tried to convert others to their own belief, or to their own scepticism. He explained what scepticism was, and told me that it was not the same thing as atheism, which he also explained. He talked about the comfort which my Grandmother had taken from her religion in her old age. But although he lived to be over seventy himself, he never departed from his view that, while a reasonable man might have faith in the future, the dogmas of the churches had no value whatever as evidence.

I went back to school from that holiday—I was fifteen—with greatly enlarged horizons. Looking back, I am struck by the intellectual honesty that would not allow my Father to equivocate with a child. I have never been able to understand those people who tell you that some modification of their own conduct is now necessary, as the children are growing up. That Christmas I had learnt three things: that good people might play cards on Sunday; that everyone should be allowed to believe what he liked; and that there were poets still alive.

Through the years of his middle age, my Father was never beaten or embittered by his almost constant material anxieties. He had, until the end, as fine a zest for life as I have ever seen. In his later years, when he acted but little himself, and became successively Secretary to the Stage Society, Manager for Lillah McCarthy and Granville-Barker at the Little and Kingsway theatres, and Barry Jackson's representative in London, he was, I think, with a home to which he was devoted, a very happy man. An event that gave him particular pleasure was an invitation to produce *The Dynasts* for the O.U.D.S.

He was extremely methodical in his affairs, and his business papers were a model of exactitude. He sent for me once in great distress. The auditors had discovered a perfectly obvious error in his Birmingham Repertory accounts. It was no use my talking; his reputation was ruined. It took me an hour to convince him that it wasn't. His office at The Kingsway, where he interviewed callers with an elaborate card-index of all living players before him, had two principal features. One was a chair, in which you sat to be interviewed. It faced the light, and had a balloon-like cushion, in which you sank to within less than a foot of the ground, holding on to the arms as on to a spar in a rough sea. The other was a cupboard in which was kept a store of apples and wine, by which the rigours of the interview might be mitigated.

He was an uncommonly good judge of a play, and of its managerial value. He was largely responsible, when *The Great Adventure* was produced, for the decision to disregard an inauspicious first fortnight, with results that were record-breaking. After the five hundredth performance in 1914, there was a celebration at the Connaught Rooms, to which I was invited. There I met Arnold Bennett for the first time. His opening words to me, much troubled in their consonants, were: 'I've often t-ried to write p-oetry. B-ut I c-an't. B-ut I b-uy it.'

Another of my Father's enthusiasms was the Trinity College of Music. He was the only man I have ever known who had literally no ear at all for music —he could never get anywhere near the tune of God Save the King. But he was treasurer and for many years on the board of that institution, and took his duties very seriously. So greatly esteemed was he, that on his death I was asked to take his place on the corporation, in order that the name might still appear in its proceedings. He took a great interest in the diction examinations, many of which he conducted. At the end, I think he spared himself too little in this work, often making long journeys and enduring much fatigue. He was, in fact, giving a lesson when he died, quite suddenly, at the age of seventy-one. He was a gentleman of great gifts and understanding.

## XXX

WHILE I was at school, my Uncle Harry was living in Oxford with his family. He had married Rose Carr, and they had three children, Grace, George, and Ruth. After his Oxford articles he had been offered a seat in George Street's London office, and there a very sound architectural instinct was influenced by a fashion for more enthusiastic than enlightened church restoration. His natural taste and draftsmanship deserved a better period. He returned to Oxford, however, well founded in his business, and enjoyed a steadily advancing practice of his own until his premature death at the age of fifty-one. He was architect, and one of the original governors, of the Oxford Theatre, and as such was associated with Arthur Bouchier in the foundation of the O.U.D.S. He and my Father were very good friends, but their occasional meetings were much given to long, receptive silences.

My Aunt Rose I found a little alarming, though she was kind to me, and I had to thank her for my first visit to the theatre, the first, that is, after the touring times with my Father. I was at her house in

Farndon Road one day for tea when she asked me if I could go to an afternoon performance of *The Merchant of Venice*. I went back to my Grandfather's at Winchester Road, and in excitement told Disciplinarian. The news produced an unpleasant effect. It was, it seemed, very undesirable for little boys to go to theatres. I was abashed, but not defeated. With great determination I succeeded in getting the cause referred to my Grandfather, even in being permitted to make my own petition. I ran upstairs, and said to him, 'Aunt Rose wants me to go to the theatre to-morrow afternoon—I suppose it's all right?' He was taken unawares, but in any case his easy-going mind would hardly have objected—I knew as much when I insisted that he should be consulted. He said 'Yes,' and I must confess that I ran downstairs again and shouted 'Yah!' in Disciplinarian's face. She said that I was exceedingly rude, and that she disapproved highly of the decision. She went up to argue the matter herself, but she had made the tactical error of letting me get in first, and I heard no more about it. My Grandfather even went so far as to send a maid round to Farndon Road to say, his compliments, and Jack could go to the theatre to-morrow.

I liked my Uncle Harry, but I did not see enough

of him to form any deep attachment. And yet I remember crying bitterly when he died in 1895, and being told by Disciplinarian that it was stupid, and hearing my Uncle Charles exclaim impatiently, 'Let the child cry if he wants to.' When my Grandfather Brown, whom I loved more than anyone else, died, I did not cry; I did not even want to. Emotion, incalculable as it is, is not more so than its expression.

Of my cousins, Grace, always poised and competent, had a manner that well became her name. With Ruth, the youngest sister, I was always on the verge of falling in love, and, at one party at least, I took heart and told her that she was the prettiest girl there. I am pleased to say that, although we were only fourteen, she was not offended. George, two years older than myself, was in later years to become, as he still is, one of my closest friends, though I was very far from suspecting it at the time.

When we were actually together we got on well enough. We acted plays, occasionally went on the river, and once he paid a visit with me to my Brown relations at Piddington. I recall a discreditable incident in my very early schooldays, when we were jointly reprimanded by his father. I happened to be spending Boat-Race day at Farndon Road, and throughout the morning George and I made the house and garden ring with a song of which the burden was—

Hurrah! Hurrah for Oxford!

Late in the afternoon news came that Cambridge had won, whereupon we sang with undiminished zest—

Hurrah! Hurrah for Cambridge!

At this point my Uncle Harry arrived home, and told us we were a disgrace to the family. I said I didn't see why, while George said he was sorry, which shows that he had a better nature than mine. But I should like his rowing friends to know that he once sang 'Hurrah for Cambridge!'

There was, however, an element of public discord in an association that privately was amiable enough. George was at the Dragon School, and the people there were considered by us at the High to be decidedly stuck up. Conscious as I was, too, of his advanced age, I could not avoid thinking that he thought himself to be a very superior person. I was convinced that he wasn't. Afterwards, when he took to the river, he attained an athletic distinction far above my class, but at school I could, figuratively, knock his head off at games. As a grown man of many accomplishments, he has always suffered from a total incapacity to say a word in his own favour, and I have no doubt that he was in fact no more given to swank in those days than is natural and healthy for small boys. But my situation was to a nicety such as to give me a sense of inferiority, which I imagined to be calculated by him. His father was richer than mine, his school more expensive, he was just an inadequate two years older than I, and he wore a crest instead of a monogram on his cap. Also, he was said to be going to a public school and perhaps to the University, while so far as I knew I wasn't going anywhere. As I say, I liked him, but he was a kind of living reproach to me, which I resented.

I conceived the idea that it would teach him and the other little Dragons if I got up a rugby fifteen from my own school which would give them a sound hiding. The challenge was laid before G. C. Vassall, who, being the sportsman that he is, accepted it, although a win for his boys against a soccer school could bring no glory, while a defeat would be ignominious. A necessary stipulation was made as to age, our seniors being a good deal older than theirs. We had a few hours of entirely unorganised practice, and went on to the field without even an elementary knowledge of the game and its rules. Mr. Vassall took firm control of the match, and prevented it from degenerating into a farce. The Dragons enjoyed an uninterrupted feast of scoring, and my misguided intentions came to a miserable end.

Another incident of a less martial character, had a more satisfactory result. One day a gentleman came into the High School playground and inquired for Drinkwater. I could not be found, and after waiting some time he went away, leaving a large parcel to be delivered to me. It contained a ravishing assortments of sweets, which put me in high favour with my friends. A week afterwards the gentleman, who was my Aunt Rose's brother and had been passing through Oxford, wrote to her asking whether George had received his present all right. Fortunately for me, he had gone to the wrong school.

On a third occasion, however, I scored a legitimate success. I went as a visitor to the Dragon School sports, and won the strangers' race. I very well remember the prize, a brown horn-handled pocket knife. And I remember, too, that my Aunt Rose was a little embarrassed by my victory, as though the family had been rather forward.

Mary Ann, Aunt Polly, was not married, and after her father's death lived with her mother at Oxford and Leamington. She was, in my recollection, one of the severer members of the family. Aunt Louisa, who was not severe, became Mrs. Champion and had several children. I remember them, when I was very small, as a friendly lot of people, in spite of some domestic strain imposed by their numbers. But one incident connected with the household stirred my dramatic imagination unforgettably. My Father took me there one day to tea, and on walking round the garden, we found my Cousin Alfred, whom I admired because he was said to be naughty, confined in a chained-off corner. I asked my Father in an awed whisper whatever could he have done. I learnt the truth as we were going home, my Father having made inquiries. Alfred, it seemed, had complained that he was insufficiently fed. This was wholly untrue, but that was the sort of naughty boy he was. That morning somebody had given him twopence. On his way home from school he had bought a haddock, and walked down the High Street of their suburb, wearing it as a sporran. This demonstration was certainly very outrageous, and so Alfred had been put, as it were, in chains. I was glad to remember that he had seemed quite unconscious of his shame. When my Father had spoken to him, his only reply was to complain that his haddock had been taken away from him.

# XXXI

AND so scrutiny, searching back from the memory of childhood into the past, comes forward to that memory again. It is, as I write, just over two hundred years since Richard Drinkwater of Tackley married Ann Pembery. And Richard begat Richard, who begat John, who begat George, who begat Albert, who begat me; their ages, seventy-odd, eighty-five, seventy-seven, sixty-five, seventy-one, and rising fifty. The Piddington descent, of which I have not been able to recover so close a record, was of the same quality. Shepherds and labourers and yeoman farmers, sometimes a keeper of fine cattle, publicans, coachmen and coachmasters, an ironmonger with a smithy behind his shop, a schoolmaster, an actor. Never rich, and in later times never so poor but they could pay scot and lot, wear good cloth, keep a bottle for company, and take a day off once in a while. Apart from one or two Drinkwaters who were farm-hands in the reign of George the Second, and my Great-uncle Thomas Brown's youngest son, who was a bank manager, I find no record of any man in either family who, whatever his station, was not his own master.

A stock of the right Puritan breed; not strait-laced or mealy-mouthed or shy of cakes and ale and pleasures, but having a rooted aversion to being pushed about by other people. They were, generation after generation, easy-going folk, so long as they were let alone. They made no exorbitant demands on life, and they seldom displayed unusual aspirations, but one and all they refused to be time-servers. With that, they were a civil, peaceable lot, with a cantankerous John but once in a century or so.

Such, then, is my inheritance, and I daresay that the biologists or the eugenists, or whoever the appropriate authorities may be, could tell me a great deal more about it than I know. At least, I dare say that they would undertake to do so, if they thought it worth while. And yet, I wonder whether they could tell me so very much after all. Does anyone really begin to understand the caprices of blood? Still more, does anyone begin to understand the caprices of character? Science may be able to track a bronchial tendency to its source, though whether the patient is thereby assisted is another matter. But who can track to its source a love of music, a distaste for meddlers, a gift for perspective, a sense of humour, intellectual courage?

The truth is that we all of us have an inordinate conceit of ourselves as judges of character. You cannot offend a man more certainly than by telling him that he is deficient in psychological insight. Accuse him of bungling a budget or precipitating a war, and although he may know that you are justified in your charge, he will smile at you. But accuse him of not understanding the intricacies of the human mind, and he will assure you that here at least you are mistaken. And yet, it is wicked to scuttle a nation's finance or to violate its peace, since these are betrayals of responsibilities that need not be undertaken. To consider the problems of character, on the other hand, is a common necessity of mankind; and to consider them inadequately is no dishonour, since to do so is the common infirmity.

Literary art has addressed itself to these problems with great pertinacity, and clearly with remarkable success. The success, however, is due not to the artist's omniscience, but to his discretion. To say that you understand character is one thing, to claim that you perceive certain truths about a character or a group of characters, quite another. The artist creates, and creation implies not only invention, but also selection. There is no character in the range of literature that is complete either in fact or in its author's intention. The subtlest creation of the greatest poet is a simpleton by comparison with the homeliest human product of nature; there is a great deal more in any railway porter—if he will not mind my saying so—than there is in Hamlet or Sordello or Soames Forsyte. This is not to disparage art in favour of nature. On the contrary, it is the distinction of art that in this respect it makes no pretence of competing with nature. The function of art is to isolate from the multiplicity of nature certain aspects of character, and present them with a hitherto unrealised lucidity. Significance is deliberately achieved at the expense of comprehensiveness. What it shows, art expresses with greater precision than nature. Or, more exactly, we should say that while an aspect or aspects of character are expressed by art, character is not expressed by nature, but comprehensively exists in nature. When we speak of art as being interpretation, we must mean just this. Character in nature is complete, but chaotic; character in art is incomplete, but clear to the perception. Some part of the formless whole has been given form, interpreted. But this operation of art can never be applied to the formless whole itself.

Indeed, we may go beyond that, and assert that the very condition of art is that it at once proclaims the artist's power and confesses his inability. Thomas Hardy in his Diary noted of Turner, 'He first recognises the impossibility of really reproducing on canvas all that is in a landscape.' The selective habit of art, which is universally acknowledged, can have but one source—the artist's desire to escape from the incomprehensibility of nature. It is the mark of the artist that, confronted by the bewildering confusion of character in nature, he is unable to endure it, and finds release in snatching some element from the vortex, and endowing it with an independent life of its own. The perfection of his vision is induced by its own imperfection. In showing us how superbly he understands the part, he reveals also that he cannot understand the whole. All art is a brand plucked from the burning.

The consequence is that character in literature must be at best a splendid attitude, an eloquent clause, seized from the fugitive activities of nature. Let art plan on as large a scale as it will, and it is nevertheless subject to the same law. The manifold life of a Tom Jones or Michael Henchard tells us far less about them than is left untold. They are much, but they are no more than the figures of a story. There they are magnificently alive, but in terms of art, not in terms of nature. Remove them from the action contrived by the artist, and straightway they fade into thin air. We may amuse ourselves by guessing what they might do in other circumstances, but the speculation is idle. Their being is designed to meet no contingencies other than those provided by the story. Nothing refreshes the spirit so surely as the escape from nature afforded by art; but escape it is.

The art of biography is as strictly bound by these conditions as the art of epic, drama, or the novel. When, however, we reflect upon character as it exists in nature, we find it to be as elusive to our speculation as it is to the processes of art. 'Man, know thyself,' is an injunction that has never been obeyed, nor can it be. How little do I know of my own character as it has been moulded by experience, and how much less when it is further involved in the endless complications of inheritance. The mazes of heredity and environment are attractively laid for the meditative mind. As we thread them, we may gather many fruits of fancy and knowledge, and they open out here and again into pleasant though passing views of a far distance. But, at the last, they are impenetrable. Even the biologist with his friend the eugenist has to turn back, the secret, whatever it may be, still undivulged.

## XXXII

AND so I cannot tell what of these old Warwickshire
and Oxfordshire people there may be in me. It has
given me a curious satisfaction, often, I am aware,
quite out of proportion to the matter, to piece together what fragments I could find of their history.
On these pursuits, the most unconsidered trifle can
be an excitement. When Mr. Page of Banbury gave
me the discoloured little card desiring Mr. Drinkwater to admit the unnamed Bearer to dinner at
four o'clock on September 25, 1832, he must have
thought my thanks strangely extravagant.

Although but the ghost of a ghost, articulated in
the echo of an echo, each of these figures has become
familiar to me. Richard, who married Ann only just
in time; Rose, who never married her Mr. Dollery
at all, though one at least of her children bore his
name, Ann Dollery Drinkwater; troublesome old
John, who was unpunctual with Mr. Loveday's
parcels; Miss Beck of Piddington since the Restoration, who found that Mr. Brown the young widower
from Standlake had such taking ways, and married
him to add four sons to his three daughters; George

[ 187 ]

who was 'much respected by all in the City of Oxford who knew him'; and Sarah his widow who left her clock standing in the kitchen to George her nephew—I affectionately acknowledge my debt to them all. And, as for the indiscretions, Thomas Hardy once wrote, in a higher key, 'That which, socially, is a great tragedy, may be in Nature no alarming circumstance.'

No emotions are more elusive than those of kinship, and yet they cut very deep. Many cordial hatreds exist between relations, but the point about them usually is that after all they are cordial. My own experience has been little troubled by such stresses. I think that if I could have known these Richards and Georges and Johns, there would have been no stresses either. The only old man whom I as a child knew intimately, my Grandfather Brown, I adored, and I am sure that I should have liked my other Grandfather, of The George, and his brother John of The White Lion. Obscure as the transmission of character may be, I know that I have from them a delight in all such things as the film of earthy chaff underfoot in a rickyard, wet brambles in October, swallows' nests on the rafters of a barn, pans of warm milk cooling on the slate slabs of a dairy, coveys in the stubble, primroses, and the plaited tails and manes of Shire horses on May Day.

# INHERITANCE

I have tried to put a sense of this inheritance into many of my poems, and into at least one dramatic character, Thomas Greenleaf of *Bird in Hand*. I have been conscious of it all my life, and with increasing pleasure as the years have gone by. I do not suppose that now a day passes but what the background of my thought is in some way conditioned by it. There are people who say that no foible seems so idle as a concern for one's ancestors. It is, I gather, implied that there is something conceited about it; which is as intelligent as to accuse a man of conceit because he likes his mother. The Chinese, who invest the emotion with worship, know better. It is an emotion that has little if anything to do with pride of family; it is as accessible to the man who has no forebears of any distinction, who, indeed, does not even know who they were, as to the descendant from half the storied houses of a kingdom. It arises from a remote, almost imperceptible, sense that this frame of ours, with its faculties, intimations, desires, fortitudes, perplexities, is in some sure though incalculable way stabilised by the undefeated courage of many generations. The Chinese are right to see in this a profoundly religious instinct. I was once talking to John Masefield gloomily about my work, when he said that it was wrong to speak so about what at worst was the best that

[ 189 ]

one could do, adding 'Always be loyal to your best moments.' And in life so many of our best moments belong to a past that was before ourselves; it is fitting that we should be loyal to them too.

It surprises me that so few people seem to set any store by little personal heirlooms, even though they have small intrinsic value. Nearly all the trifles that cram the curiosity shops once had what might still have been a living association, which no one has thought it worth while to preserve. How many of the collectors who will pay large sums for what are called historical relics even pause to reflect that their own grandfathers were part of history too? I am as fond as any of these tangible tokens of the famous, but I would not exchange the silver buttons from that old John Drinkwater's coaching coat for the buttons worn by Marlborough at Blenheim. Last summer my Aunt Mary, the widow of Charles, my Mother's brother, gave me some things that belonged to my Grandfather Brown at Winchester Road. They were a white parian statuette of Wellington, Samuel Cousins's steel engraving of Landseer's 'Return from Hawking,' a group of bronze mantelshelf ornaments—candlesticks, spill-holders, and a model of Napoleon's tomb—and a dessert service of rich amber colour, charmingly decorated with delicately tinted flowers, each piece bearing the appropriate imprint 'Bouquet' on the back. This last is probably worth a little money, but the rest no doubt would have been put together in an odd lot and sold under the hammer for a few shillings. It was Oscar Wilde who said of some unfortunate man that he knew the price of everything and the value of nothing.

Mr. Gilbert Cannan once wrote of me, 'Mr. Drinkwater is English, almost myopically English.' The friendly indictment gave me great pleasure. I have no disclaimer to put in. So far as I have been able to trace my descent on both sides, there has been no drop of any but English blood brought into the family for over two hundred years. And Midland English at that, with an area of no more than two counties. Although I have spent most of my life in the large cities, I still at times in my speech turn a word with an Oxfordshire burr, not, I think, just picked up in childhood, but inherited from old village-greens and inn-yards.

English, and bred of a stock as far inland as it is possible for an Englishman to be. Which accounts, perhaps, for an indifference that I suppose no Englishman should confess. I am no seaman. If the weather, the lodgings, the sands and the company are good, I can enjoy a holiday at the sea-side like other people. But for the sea as a trade or an adventure I have no yearning whatever. Ships at sea are beautiful, but I prefer to watch them from the shore. The spectacle of Arnold Bennett in a yachting cap always filled me with melancholy sensations. The sea is all right, and it has done us a lot of good, but I never hear it calling me. I don't avoid it, but if I never saw it again I shouldn't miss it. If one wanted to be nasty one would submit that there must be something fishy about an element that can sink to the dreary futility of the mid-Atlantic.

I feel much the same about mountains. I have seen the Rockies and the Alps, the Balkans and the Pyrenees, the Cumbrians and the Cambrians, the Pennines and the Olympics, and several others which I forget. I have even climbed up some of them, to great heights, my best being 14,000 feet at the Tennessee Pass on the Union Pacific Railroad. Of course, they are magnificent, and Hail Caledonia-Stern and Wild, and all that. I would never speak disrespectfully of a mountain. But I don't need mountains. Although the Olympics at sunrise are superb—a scene, as I can testify, that would be the despair of Herr Reinhardt—give me summer-time on Bredon.

But the hedges, the lanes, the pastures, the spinneys and the streams that Shakespeare knew are another matter. If I am away from these for long I grow restless. And, among them, no season or weather comes amiss. Snow or halcyon, floods or drought, noon or twilight, winter or summer, that quiet, reticent landscape never becomes either tedious or importunate. It is a comfortable (Oh, comfortable friar), sustaining friend, unexacting, and infinitely fertile to those who are patient. I find that I have lived with all its moods in my poetry; with the sea and the mountains hardly at all.

# XXXIII

Therefore all seasons shall be sweet to thee,
Whether the summer clothe the general earth
With greenness, or the redbreast sit and sing
Betwixt the tufts of snow on the bare branch
Of mossy apple-tree, while the night thatch
Smokes in the sun-thaw; whether the eave-drops fall
Heard only in the trances of the blast,
Or if the secret ministry of frost
Shall hang them up in silent icicles,
Quietly shining to the quiet moon.

THE 'Dear Babe' whom Coleridge addressed in these perfect lines was cradled among 'lakes and shores and mountain crags,' and it was from these that he was to learn 'the lovely shapes and sounds intelligible of that eternal language' to whose gospel the poet committed him. But it will be noted that the imagery in these closing lines is not of grandeur, but all of tranquillity. The scene has moved from the crags to the garden round the cottage-eaves. An examination of the Lake poets in this respect would show that their majestic surroundings never held their attention for long from the homelier foreground. Men may climb to the mountain-tops, but they live in the valleys.

The landscape of my inheritance might have been in every way a natural inspiration for Coleridge's lines. They move with a tenderness that accords beautifully with its own.

*Therefore all seasons shall be sweet to thee—*

and this is how it is:

Spring in the Midlands, as elsewhere, has a provoking way of being true to form, in spite of hopes that revive annually. April ought to be such a lovely month, and seldom is. Chill rains and east winds always seem to drop in as though it were by accident, and in spite of them we are credulous enough to go on backing to-morrow to come to a sense of the season's grace. But the wise Englishman learns that the April season is, in fact, graceless—or at least that its grace is not of the kind with which illusion has endowed it. The truth is that, winter over, what most people really expect is not spring, but summer. They look for full leafage with the first buds, and are impatient of the slow transfiguration. The English spring, rightly known, is as adorable as English youth; but, like youth, it is wayward, bracing, sometimes a little harsh, not mature, but unquiet and urgent. It is foolish to forget that it is not yet the time of mellow nights and full-throated ease.

But take our Midland spring for what it is, and how exquisite are the rewards. The warm south may so seldom visit us as to warm us to a glow of surprise when it does, but for all its inclemencies there is no other season of the year that has so enchantedly, so poignantly, the joy of discovery. It is, after all, the prime. What ravishing wonders they are, the first primrose on the bank, the first violet under the beeches, perhaps a white violet even, the first blue of a hedgesparrow's egg, the cuckoo's note, the transparency of green suddenly come upon the ploughlands. And then those fantastic lambs, with legs that successfully defy probability, fluttering about a new earth like woolly shuttlecocks. Milton's hungry sheep looked up and were not fed, but here a more natural consideration is shown.

Everything is virginal: sight, scent, and sound. The larches and the blackthorns have a purity of colour that never seems to be quite recaptured by the later year. The spring flowers, the cowslips and wood-violets, surprise us with a fragrance so delicate that it would be absorbed unnoted by the perfumes of summer, and the first mist of bluebells or graeggles in a glade can be matched only by the azure of dawn. The plumage and the song of the birds are now bright and lyrical in their mating tones. Even the palate is more fastidious, and the touch quicker to texture, than at other seasons. As the sap rises, earth and all its creatures stir again to the miraculous discovery of power.

Early in the year, for the first lambs are dropped in snow-time, the shepherds relax their care, and, with the harvests sown, labour on the land goes on at an easy pace. Not idly, nor unanxiously, for there are the cattle night and morning, the orchards to dress, the waggons—still as lovely as they were when they took Herrick's girls to the Maypole—to be painted, the multifarious gear to be repaired, oiled, ground, polished, put generally in order. Much of it even to-day is the same as it was in those far days at Piddington and Drayton. The old hand-flail, two ash-poles loosely hinged by a leather thong, is obsolete, but this year I saw a man sowing a ten-acre field, striding the furrows rhythmically with a wide bin held firmly to his waist with one hand, while the other threw out a spray of seed, left-right, left-right, I am sure to a ditty that I could not hear, like sailors hauling up the anchor. He was not white, but clad in a reach-me-down from the local shop; otherwise he was the husbandman of Thomson's 'Spring,' published in 1728—

White through the neighbouring fields the sower
  stalks,
With measured step, and liberal throws the grain
Into the faithful bosom of the ground.

Spring, so rich, so assured in its promise, so glowing in its passion, is fittingly the festival of caprice,
as it is of love. Any morning, after a sunset of mild
airs and late song, you may wake to find the puddles
in the cart-tracks thinly sheeted with ice, or the paddock powdered with snow. Civilization, they say,
marches, but we have learnt nothing since Boadicea
that can ward us against these late frosts. 'Nipped
in the bud' has become a commonplace of our language. Hardly a spring passes but levies toll of this
kind. And yet, year by year, the hazards are survived, 'the buried bulbs' break into flame, abundance
conquers stealth, and summer comes.

## XXXIV

IF spring makes much of its moods, promising only
to deceive, and mostly affecting a mask that is
double-faced, the transformation to summer, when it
comes, is almost instantaneous. Even while your
back has been turned, you will find that the trees
and hedges have become screens that the light can
no longer pierce, masses of glowing green with heavy
underfolds of shadow. Hourly the earth augments
itself in clouds and billows and plumes of green,
and before you know where you are the lilacs are
out, and a pink blush mantles the dark foliage of the
chestnuts.

It is impossible now to keep pace with the flowers;
they are as many in their constellations as the stars.
Every meadow and lane and wood is thick with
them, some of them so common that we hardly remember that they are flowers at all. The young
crops seem to grow by inches daily, and the blossom
falls from the fruit-trees, leaving clusters of tiny
apples and plums and pears. The clover-tops begin
to form, and there is a ruffle of grey as the wind
turns the under-sides of the bean-leaves.

# INHERITANCE

The shorn sheep are cooling in the pastures by the time June is in, and soon the cattle come to stay longer at their watering-places than is necessary to quench their thirst. The hedgerows are lustrous with may and the pale honey flowers of the nettles, and a shimmer of heat vibrates to the sound of grasshoppers in the growing hay. The whitethroat is in full song, and, if your ear is quick enough, you may catch the nightingale's notes in the chorus of noon. All day long the swifts soar and dive through the air in the great arcs of their miraculous flight. The window-panes are a buzzing of flies. As you walk along, you may suddenly find on a bough, within a few feet of you, a young thrush or blackbird, very solemn, and hoping that he has escaped your notice, since he has not yet taken sufficient breath for a further flight.

And then hay-harvest comes on, with its great stone jars of beer, and sunbonnets, and destruction of larks' nests. Not stout Cortez with his eagle eyes stared more anxiously at the Pacific, than these folk now watch the horizons for the cloud no bigger than a man's hand. The weather, always a care, becomes a daily apprehension until the swaths, kept loose and ventilated by the tedding forks, have sucked in the last sweetness of the sun and been safely ricked. Hay must be crisp and springy if the haycocks are to keep fresh and wholesome. Once let it get sodden, or even ropy, and you can never be sure what will happen afterwards. The damp once in the cut grass is as difficult to exorcise as the devil. And so, that anxious watch all through making-time. So often and so suddenly has the thunder piled up into a clear sky, to break upon that immemorial scene in torrents of misfortune if not disaster. A good crop after this may hardly be worth carrying, and if carried, there will be a fear of ricks firing until autumn has passed.

But, if fortune holds good, there is a perfection of health in haymaking. Here is earth giving with her most lavish bounty, not returning the seed a hundred-fold, but yielding abundance for no sowing. And the hay-harvesters, men and women, glow with a beauty and vigour that belong to this season alone. There is nothing quite like the tan to be seen on the arms and faces and throats in a hayfield. The pigmentation of the sun has worked slowly and naturally into the texture of the skin, and gives a tone, at once animated and rough, that seems to belong to the flesh, and is sought in vain by the fashionable beauties of both sexes who are assiduous in its pursuit though Caliban's south-west blow on them and blister them all o'er.

And then, at summer's end, comes that other and

[ 201 ]

yet richer harvest, the festival of the year, loading
the barns and rickyards with wheat and beans and
oats and barley. Again all minds are on the weather,
but even the vagaries of our English climate have
to be unusually violent to defeat at last the consum-
mation of harvest-home. On fine days, from early
morning often into the moonlit night, the land is in
a state of unceasing activity. Machinery has brought
in change, and I suppose the immigrant Irish labourers no longer begin to drift into the Oxfordshire farms for casual employment when August
Bank Holiday has gone. But the reaping and bind-
ing and gleaning still go on, and there is still the
continual procession of waggons between the fields
and the farmsteads. It is true everywhere that an
alteration of methods does far less to alter the nature
of things than we are apt to suppose; and it is true
particularly of this rural life. A Piddington wheat-
field with its poppies looks to-day what it did to my
Grandfather Brown when he was a boy there a hundred years ago. It is harvested with the same anxieties, it goes by the same roads often to the same
barns, and it is ground to the same flour. In fact,
the same designs are turned to the same ends; the
only change is here and there in the practical econ-
omies of the process, with what net gain I must
leave others to decide.

But then this Midland country, in spite of its show sights, is in many places remarkably tenacious still of tradition and old custom. The twenty-ninth of May is still Shic-Shac Day. Thomas Hardy in a letter to Edmund Gosse wrote: 'Oak-apple Day is exotic; "Sic-Sac Day" or "Shic-Sac Day" being what the peasantry call it.' That may be true of Dorset, but in the Boscobel country it is Shic-Shac. There are places in Warwickshire where the goldfinches, building in the apple-orchards, are still called proud tailors. And about the outlying farms you may still find men who make it seem natural enough that there was once in Warwickshire a Midsummer Night's Dream.

## XXXV

THE transition from summer to autumn is very much more gradual than that from spring to summer. We can never foretell to a day or a week when this latter will be made, but it is nearly always made on an instant and decisively, the whole contour and temper of nature being suddenly metamorphosed. Summer glides into autumn imperceptibly, and the advent of the fall has almost to be announced by some agreed formula: the fields are now stubble, therefore it is autumn.

Given a little time to assert itself, however, the season of mists and mellow fruitfulness has, perhaps, a more composed personality than any other. The only fragrance that approaches the spring flowers in subtlety is that of the orchards in full fruit, with windfalls lying among the grass and dock-leaves before the ladders and baskets have been brought out. And when the ladders are up and the baskets heaped, what an Aladdin's wonder of gem-like colours is there, gold and topaz and ruby and purple, emerald and russet.

Slowly the trees are streaked and stained with the

same prodigality of hue, nature blending her infinite variety and gradation of colour to unerring harmony. Nowhere is the splendour of decay so magnificent as in foliage. And the trees, too, have now another bounty. The hazels and filberts, brown and ripe and gleaming, slip from their hods at every stirring of the bough. The walnuts, tumbling to earth with a little muted thud, almost like the rise of a trout, lie half-buried among their own leaves, which we turn with a foot to find the clean shells, loosened now in their split husks. Sometimes the husks are left to hang shrivelled and silhouetted on the branches into early winter. There is another nut-bearing tree that few people in England esteem as such. Beeches in the congestion of the wood, I find, seldom produce fruit with any kernel, but a pocketful gathered from the beechmast of a good tree standing in the open has often a very delicate flavour.

Cider is a good name, but to the men of Warwick and Oxford it has never had the reputation as a drink which it enjoys in the neighbouring counties of Somerset and Gloucester. The apples and the presses are auspicious, and Thomas Hardy's immortal scene in *The Woodlanders* has given prestige to a beverage that some of us find but a stomach-achey affair. I remember a Birmingham professor who, on being told that a colleague's wife had given birth to twins, a boy and a girl, observed after an abstracted pause, 'No—I recall no authority for the phenomenon in the classics.' Similarly, I recall no authority for cider in Shakespeare, whereas ale, which we favour, has been much celebrated in song since before Noah was a sailor.

An especial satisfaction of autumn are the mushrooms. They are good to eat, but better still to find. Tradition has it that you must be out early for them, but in secluded places the time does not matter. White though they are against the green, they somehow conceal themselves as cunningly as a brood of young lapwings along a stone wall at the approach of an intruder. Not only the mushrooms in long grass, but those, the better sort usually, that come up short and crisp on the sparsely-grown ridges and furrows, where a clump of them a few yards away can stare you in the face unseen. A good basket should contain no buttons, which should be left for a later gathering, and no gills that have staled from pink through brown to unquestionable black; but that is a counsel of perfection. When mushrooming it needs unusual self-control to rise above the code of finding's keeping.

There is one particular bird-note in autumn that is heard at no other time. Whether the note itself is actually different, or whether the atmosphere gives it a special quality I am not sure, but there is no sound in nature like that of starlings chattering in a tree on a September morning. Chattering is not the right word, suggesting as it does something aimless and irregular. This sound has a steady metronomic pulse, and vibrates like the note of a locust, or the rapid staccato of partridge wings in flight. It is even more nearly the echo of some mechanical noise, such as that of a lawn-mower in diminuendo. What the starlings mean by it I have no idea. It is not a mating-song. But then, of all our common birds, the starlings are, perhaps, the most incalculable. Living in large flocks, there is little evidence to support the view held by some authorities that they migrate overseas. But, within Great Britain, inland migration takes place on a large scale. The colony does not move in one flock, but in a succession of smaller units. I have watched these passing in a steady stream northwards, at intervals of two or three hundred yards, for over an hour; there must have been millions of birds. Perhaps the simmering in the autumn trees denotes preparation for some such movement. In any case it belongs, as I know it, to the autumnal tones, to mornings when the dew hangs on the gossamer long after sunrise.

As the leaves fall and the days draw in, a weaker

noon draws off the damps from earth, and the hollows and undergrowth begin to grow sodden. The ditches, drained almost to their beds, fill up again, and on windless days mists lie upon the fields at dawn and dusk. Slowly again the timber of the trees and hedges traces its structure against the light, and a new layer of leaf-mould settles on to the carpet of the woods. The nests that defied our search in June are conspicuous in every bush. The swallows, perpetually in motion since April, cluster on the roofs, stirred now only by strange little expectant movements. This goes on for days, and then one morning they are gone. Autumn, the fall of the year, itself is passing for winter to prepare another spring.

## XXXVI

I AM one of the fortunate people who, when all the delights of spring and summer and autumn are spent, can still look forward to winter as, on the whole, the most satisfactory season of the year.

I am well aware of all the opprobrious things that are said about our winter climate. Since they obsess our conversation, it is impossible not to be aware of them. But let me say at once that I enjoy bad weather, or at least what other people choose to call bad weather. I don't call it that; I call it just weather, as I call any other weather weather. Of course, if you want it to be eighty in the shade and never to see anything but a sky interminably blue in winter, then you ought to go somewhere else. But as an Englishman I have been bred through many generations to endure English weather, and since I can endure it without discomfort, I enjoy it, and all of it. I exclude city fogs, but they are really the prerogative of London, and even so they would be rather amusing if they were not so damned inconvenient. In any case, they do not trouble us in the Midlands, nor in the country does the occasional high temperature of July become offensive as it can in Bond Street and Soho. For the rest, I think the English climate is the best in the world, winter and all.

I can well understand visitors being upset by it; those hardy pioneers from the Middle-West, for example, who blanch if you propose to open a window and like the pillow on the steampipe side of the bed. I don't blame them. I should be like that if I had been bred to a climate so violent that you have to move into an ice-chest for the summer and into an hermetically sealed hot-air compartment for the winter. That kind of thing takes all the natural resistance out of a man. There is only one thing to do with weather like that—escape from it. But the normal Englishman has learnt to face his less convulsive weather, and has grown hardened to it in consequence. Whatever its defects, there is not a day in the year when it keeps him indoors, or even makes it seriously uncomfortable to go out. He may wear light clothes or warm, but he has neither to strip nor dress himself up like a polar bear. And if he is sensible, he takes his weather as it comes, and enjoys it all.

So that if it rains in winter I put on a mackintosh, and if it freezes I walk a little faster. And people talk a lot of nonsense about the sun. They tell you they can't live without it. Of course they can't—nor can I. But I don't think the less of the sun because it doesn't turn up every morning like the milkman. For myself, the sun is definitely one of the good things of which I can have too much. I worship as much of it as I get in England—there are many glorious days all the year round when one really does worship—and I don't want any more. Uninterrupted sunshine would bleach my mind.

And let me add that if this country ever gives up its open fireplaces in favour of some synthetic caloric, it will have squandered one of its most agreeable social assets. A cold room and a warm fire is the last refinement of creature comfort. And if the room be a bedroom, and to the fire be added, when the thermometer is well below 32° F., a hot-water bottle in default of the more heroic warming-pan, then the comfort becomes epicurean. Mary Stuart thought the Scots barbarians when she remembered the French court. But these barbarian palates have a way of being finer than those of sophistication. And the Scot, a master of essential taste, likes his porridge very hot, and his milk, taken in alternate spoonfuls, very cold.

There are hours when the worst rage of winter weather—Chaucer's wintres weders—is the better the worse it is. Those country nights, when wind and rain beat frozen on to the windows, and all within is snug with logs blazing and perhaps even a muller in the fire—who with Prospero's wand would bid the elements be still?

The holly shines brighter even than the hips, though not so bright as the haws. To-day still, when so many ladies and more gentlemen weekly achieve Press notoriety by failing to break a record, this romantic berry stands for Christmas, and there are many people, myself, I am proud to say, among them, who still spend Christmas Eve decorating a Christmas tree with innumerable presents and baubles, bought, I am not so proud to say, chiefly from Mr. Woolworth who turned The Red Lion out of Banbury. Richard Drinkwater of Tackley had a little Christmas tree in 1729, when Ann was bearing that first daughter. I have no proof of the fact, but nobody is in a position to dispute my belief. Christmas trees, I am sure, have been long cherished by my ancestors. They, no doubt, went out and cut them down in the nearest copse; I go out and pay five shillings to my green grocer. But I pay it in a ritualistic fervour—there is no crown in the year that I spend with more satisfaction. And when other members of the family secretively attach to the branches packages that I know bear my own name, I am in a twitter of excitement. If the higher journalism is pleased to consider this sentimental in the manner of Sir James Barrie or Mr. Galsworthy or Mr. Milne, it is very welcome to its pleasure.

A particular delight of the country winter in England is the weekly visit to the neighbouring town, population perhaps four thousand. Shopping there has a zest in the bustling cold that Regent Street can never provide. You can almost see the bleak wind nipping along the pavements, sheering up to the game and turkeys hanging in the poulterer's shopfront, biting the policeman's ears. Greetings ring out on the frosty air with an impetus that reconciles even the vicar with the agnostic. It is on record that one December morning long ago in Bicester, the Bishop of Oxford stopped a celebrated pagan poet to wish him the compliments of the season and thank him for his verses.

In winter they plough, and hounds go to cover.

Over the broad hill creeps a beam,
    Like hope that gilds a good man's brow;
And now ascends the nostril-steam
    Of stalwart horses come to plough.

Ye rigid Ploughman, bear in mind
    Your labour is for future hours:
Advance—spare not—nor look behind—
    Plough deep and straight with all your powers.

Though with less philosophic intent than Horne advocates, the ploughman does go forward with all his powers, deep enough when stones let him, and straight too, which is no small matter of skill, especially if you should have a jibbing horse in front. It is, in an old Oxfordshire word, unkid difficult to drive a field of level furrows with a quiet team; a jibber may mar all. And once in a while both of them may go east and west to hounds in full cry.

For a pack over the land intoxicates everything. The watch-dogs nearly throttle themselves on their chains, the cattle scurry, the sheep stiffen like wooden things out of Noah's Ark. Threshers high up on the rick wave their forks and shout incoherently tally-ho! gone-away! ooo-eee! as though they had seen every fox in the kingdom, when they have seen none. Passengers on the highroad, afoot or awheel, turn incontinently in their tracks and dash off in a direction to which no one has directed them. Birds and hares and rabbits behave as though the primeval stoat had been let loose, and strange incantations rise from all quarters of the landscape. The hunt pours on, and in a minute all again is still; the ploughman goes forward, deep and straight.

It starts in November, that 'glorious, sloppy, poachy, wet-me-through month' so beloved of Surtees. When the partridges are beginning to fly wild, the Bicesters are out on the fast, open country that was dear to the handsome Lord Valentia in my particular Tom Brown's schooldays. I have already alluded to the ethics of fox-hunting; it has none. But surely nothing so bad was ever such good going. Going, perhaps, is the just word; for the sport, I suspect, is not likely long to survive. When it goes, a cruel thing will go, but with it will go also a microcosm of much that is best in English character.

By the calendar, winter ends with January, but in fact it usually sees March in. The second month of the year, however, discovers the snowdrop. The botanist calls it 'a genus of plants of the natural order *Amaryllis*, with bell-shaped flower arising from a spathe, bulbous root, two leaves and one single-flowered leafless-stem.' For the rest of us it is the first, and incontestable, token of spring.

## XXXVII

SUCH are the aspects and incidents of the year that most readily come to my mind. The habit for these things was formed in childhood, and was, indeed, part—a very valuable part—of my inheritance. My fathers who were before me left me no land, but, I thank them, they left me a love of it. I have, I hope they would think, honoured the debt in *The Midlands*, *Burning Bush*, and a score of poems besides.

My Grandfather died at Winchester Road in 1895, when he was over seventy and I was under fourteen. He had been much the most considerable person in my life. I could remember him as something friendly even before I went to live with him. At the time of Queen Victoria's Jubilee, in 1887, when I was five, I was staying with him, and he lifted me up to his shoulders so that I could see some procession over the heads of the people in the Parks. It was in his house that I had lain abed on the eve of my tenth birthday, persuaded that if I could keep awake till midnight I should find myself growing suddenly taller like Alice. It was there that I had written my first poem, for which I got a medal (bronze) from *Little Folks:*

There was a little Chinaman
Whose name was Hi Pang Te.
He had as nice a pig-tail
As you could wish to see.
Now of this little Chinaman,
I have no more to say,
Except that he lived in China-land,
Some two thousand miles away.

Disciplinarian was not pleased about the medal—
she thought it likely to set me up above myself. But
even at that tender age, and in the flush of success,
I had a suspicion that the poem was not really a
very good one; I was conscious particularly of its
impotent conclusion. With it, happily, the springs
of my juvenile inspiration ran dry.

Less distinguished had been the day when I was
taken to bed with a colic, brought on by a surfeit of
green gooseberries. They had been presented to me
by a school friend whose father was a market-
gardener. I arrived home in a state of great agita-
tion, and was led upstairs in contortions of pain.
As I lay on my back, frequent relays of hot bricks
wrapped in flannel were placed upon my stomach,
and my indisposition passed off. I told my school
friend that he was a sneak, which was unreasonable.

Of the close and daily companionship with my
Grandfather I have already spoken. My Grand-

mother, who had been a Miss Stone before she married him, I never knew. Towards the end, without any specific illness, he grew enfeebled, and just faded away. One evening I played a rubber of cribbage with him as usual, was given a penny, and said good-night without a sense of anything unusual. The next morning I was told that he had died in his sleep.

I was sent out to Piddington to take the news to his brother Thomas. I went by train to Bicester and walked the other four miles. On my journey I felt vaguely important as the bearer of grave tidings, and I felt vaguely sorry that my Grandfather was dead. But, although I was no longer quite a small child, I was still too young to realise the full impact of that irrevocable word. And the strange thing is, or perhaps in the light of most human experience not so strange after all, that as I sat in the train, and then walked along the road by Blackthorn, I experienced no strong feelings of any kind. I was not numbed or anything like that. It was merely as though nothing out of the way had happened. Nor was I afterwards conscious of any real distress. And yet I do not think that affection between a little boy and an old man could have been deeper.

When I reached the Piddington farm, my Great-aunt Sarah met me in the porch. I said 'Grandpa has died,' and she replied, 'I thought so.' I heard her go into the parlour and say, 'Thomas, John's dead.' I followed her, and found the last of the old Browns sitting on a high-backed chair, smoking his long pipe, with a newspaper fallen across his knees. 'Well, boy,' was all he said.

That evening I saw my Grandfather, the first dead person I had seen. I don't know how it happened, but I was taken into the room by my Aunt Rose, who knelt down by the bed and was very quiet, and then got up and kissed his forehead before leaving. I wondered whether I ought to kiss him too, but nothing was said, so I didn't. I thought he looked thin but very beautiful, and, although I felt rather shy, I was not at all frightened.

I don't think I can have gone to the funeral since I cannot remember it. He left his estate, which included the Cornmarket business but was not a large one, to his son Charles, my Mother's share having been mortgaged by the support and education of my sister and myself. His will provided, however, that a hundred pounds for each of us should be used by trustees to finish our schooling. My sister had already gone to her Belgian convent, and I now went to the Rev. H. R. Hall's house on the Banbury Road, where about a dozen of the High School boys lived as boarders. I remained there for three terms.

# XXXVIII

My consistent failure to distinguish myself at school said little for the principle that all work and no play makes Jack a dull boy, for I played with great pertinacity. In the holidays I ran a football team—it was hardly an eleven—which played on a piece of waste-ground with cricket-stumps for goalposts. I made myself captain of a group of what to-day would be boy-scouts, which performed evolutions of a Red Indian character in the Headington Quarries. I was always getting up paper-chases, in which as hare I chose the muddiest routes available in order to create a good impression when we got back. On one of these excursions I smoked my first cigarette. It had a very peculiar flavour, but did not make me sick. To-day, if I stop smoking during a cold, the first cigarette afterwards has exactly the same taste. I did not smoke at school, however. When I left to take up business at the age of fifteen and a half, I went into a tobacconist's shop at Nottingham and bought two cigarettes for a penny. My Father had exacted no promises, but had told me that it would be better if I did not smoke until I was eighteen.

Independence, however, tempted me, and I bought my two cigarettes. I then thought better of it, and took no tobacco again until my eighteenth birthday, when I shocked my Father's economic prudence by buying both a pipe and a pouch out of the same week's money.

Of two minor accomplishments I was a master. One was 'conkers.' I had a chestnut which I had baked—this was legitimate—and then laid up in storage. When it was brought out into action on a string it was invincible, and 'conked' or 'conquered' —I am not sure which is the correct term—some thousands of its rivals. The total mounted like this; if your conker conked a conker that had previously conked ten other conkers, your conker added eleven to its tally of victims. My champion, which was a playground classic, finally came to grief when I missed my aim and hit a stone buttress instead. On a technical knockout another boy's very mean and soft sort of a little conker acquired my beauty's title, which however it had speedily to surrender to some other weakling. Mine was probably the most efficient chestnut on record. It grew in Norham Gardens, and I can remember its shape now.

My other mastery was in the marble-ring. We played the large-ring game, known I believe as the 'first-tor-ringums-lag' variety. If I worked it out, I am sure I could recall what the precise meaning of that incantation was—in fact I do recall it as I write, but it makes no matter. I started with twenty marbles, little blue and brown and yellow and red clay balls, which cost a penny, and one agate which was expensive and cost a halfpenny. In the course of time my twenty became several hundreds, and I had enough agates to fill a solitaire board. This actually was the case, and, on one occasion, miserably.

Disciplinarian had found an empty board somewhere, and space by space I supplied it with tors of the species known as bubblysees—they were the green glass balls taken from lemonade bottles. One day, returning home from school at tea-time even later than usual, I decided on the way home to placate the wrath to come by giving her, en bloc, the five new bubblysees that I had just won. She refused them, whereupon I went out and in a pet threw them broadcast into the garden. She asked me what I had done; I told her. Then would I please go out and find them before taking tea, and what wickedness I should be up to next she couldn't tell.

In more serious athletic pursuits, however, I also had some success, by the not very exacting standards of the school. I got my cricket and football colours as, I think, the youngest member of both teams, the latter award being attended by a very embarrassing circumstance. I had been told privately beforehand of the Captain's intention to put my name on the colours list at the end of the term. I knew that the question of the price of a shirt would provoke a crisis at home, and very indiscreetly I asked a colours who was leaving whether he would sell his cheap. Somehow this came to the knowledge of the Captain, who stopped me in the playground and asked if I could call to see him at his home that evening. His name was Geikie, and he lived in St. Giles's. I went, and he asked me what I meant by taking things for granted like that. When the time came for me to buy a colours shirt, he would let me know about it. I said I was most frightfully sorry, and that I honestly hadn't seen what an ass I was making of myself. He was then very nice about it, and said that although I was an ass it was all right. He is now, I believe, a dentist. I hope he has all the practice that he could desire; and I hope that whoever it was who told him about the shirt has the toothache.

At the school sports I was never old enough to have a chance in the open events, but I did well in the junior sprints and jumps. One year, indeed, so well that I began to fancy myself, and persuaded my Grandfather to let me enter for the junior 120 yards' at the City Sports on Bank Holiday. I trained

INHERITANCE

assiduously for this, and often stopped to admire the
handsome travelling-clock that was displayed for
some time before the meeting among the other prizes
in a jeweller's window. When the day came, I found
that my school exploits had resulted in my being
penalized four yards. As we lined up I found myself
behind what seemed to be a solid phalanx of competitors, some of whom had ten yards start. Even if
my speed had been equal to the odds, I could never
have penetrated the mass that sped in front of me
along the Iffley Road straight. In any case, I was
nowhere, and later in the afternoon I had the mortification of seeing the clock presented to the son of the
porter at my own school. I went home severely chas-
tened.

One triumph, however, was, and remains, securely
mine. In the same year that C. B. Fry at Iffley broke
the world's record for the long jump, I on the same
ground broke the long jump record for boys under
fourteen at the Oxford High School. It is true that
he jumped twenty-three feet five inches, and I only
jumped fifteen feet eight, but while the former distance may be allowed to be a remarkable one for
anybody to cover, I may thirty-five years after be
forgiven for claiming that the latter is a remarkable
one for a boy of thirteen to cover. Moreover, since
then other people have jumped more than twenty-

Oxford High School sports (University Running Ground),
1896.  Long jump, under 14, to Drinkwater: 15 ft. 8 in.

three feet five, whereas no boy under fourteen at the Oxford High School has jumped more than fifteen feet eight. And now the junior age limit has been raised to fifteen, so that my record for the under fourteen event remains on the school registers for ever. I saw it the other day, beautifully immune against the red-ink pen that strikes out the glories that perish. I am afraid that hardly anything else in my life has been as final as that.

## XXXIX

My particular friend at Hall's was Norman Kent. We were both precariously in the Fifth under Belcher, and being senior boys of the house we shared a private study. The principal advantage of this was not that it enabled us to work better, as this was not our ambition, but that it contained a slow combustion stove in which we could bake potatoes. Kent did more work than I; that is to say, he occasionally did a little. He also had an incomparable talent for covering himself with ink. I have since known many children adepts at inky fingers, but none who could approach Kent's facility in a broader technique. He could apply ink to his mouth, his nose, even to his ears and neck, with an easy impartiality. I liked Kent, and was, too, dependent on him, as when he gave his mind to it he was far quicker than I at Latin prose and such, but this disordered relish for ink annoyed me. I was an untidy and often a shabby little boy, but I never could bear dirt of any kind on my face or hands. Sticky fingers were a torment that I would not endure, and the only fight I ever had at school was with a boy who put a squashed plum in my pocket. I daresay my fastidiousness was priggish, but Kent inky was a distress to me. Otherwise we got on famously together.

I don't know what possessed us to do it, but one day we decided that the time had come for us to wear stand-up collars. Accordingly, we bought one each. The next morning our sartorial bounce escaped the notice of the House authorities, but by no means that of Belcher. After prayers he called us up to his desk. 'Kent and Drinkwater, what have you got round your necks?' 'Collars, sir.' 'I see. Please turn round.' We did so, facing the form. 'Kent and Drinkwater would like you to see their collars.' He left us for several moments to our discomfiture; then—'Blockheads. Go to your places.'

In the Fifth, Kent and I were not a success, being bottom and bottom but one with alternating but otherwise fixed fortunes. But our seniority made us swells at Hall's, and our study was the rendezvous for the choicer spirits of the House. Half a dozen of us agreed one evening that we would each write to a famous cricketer, saying what a fine cricketer he was, and hoping for the best. I, holding that not failure but low aim was crime, chose W. G. Grace, and got nothing. Others got an autograph, but one boy—was it Finch?—writing to Kortright, who for two overs probably had a yard on anyone in the great succession of fast bowlers, excited general and ill-dissembled envy by receiving an old bat. In a Gentleman-Players match at Lords, by the way, I once saw Kortright knock Johnny Brigg's middle wicket out of the ground first ball with a full toss.

Kent became, and I believe still is, a chaplain in the Navy, serving through the war on the battleship that bore his own name. Like myself, he was very partial to a glutinous kind of pop-corn, which was a cheap and satisfying sweetmeat of those days. We were on good terms with the pretty young lady-housekeeper, whose name was Patty, and she used sometimes to give us unlawful rations from the larder. Not that we went short of food at table; Mrs. Hall, having children of her own, saw to it that we were well fed. I still remember the relish of a regular weekly breakfast in winter, when we each had a large square roll—it was really rather a small tin-loaf than a roll—steaming hot, and a boiled egg. Nevertheless, our appetites were always equal to Patty's liberality, and many delicacies were spirited upstairs at bedtime. One night I had acquired a substantial slice of cold bread-and-butter pudding, which I was eating furtively after lights were out. A sudden step at the door took me unaware, and I thrust my spoils hastily under the pillow, with disgusting results.

The step that startled me was that of A. L. Corbett, the soccer blue and our assistant house-master. He was very popular, and but seldom made these unexpected calls. Once, however, I was, in my own opinion at least, the innocent victim of his displeasure. We slept four or five in a dormitory, and often at night played games of the kind in which one player has to go out of the room. This being impossible, he undertook to hear nothing until the others were ready. On one such occasion, I had my head under the bed-clothes, my fingers in my ears, and was singing:

'Last night down our alley came a toff,'

when the door opened. I learnt afterwards that the following concerted dialogue took place:

| | |
|---|---|
| *Corbett* | Who's making that row? |
| *Drinkwater* | 'Fair old geeser with a nasty cough' |
| | |
| *Corbett* | Drinkwater! Stop that noise! |
| *Drinkwater* | 'Sees my missus, takes his topper off,' |
| | |
| *Corbett* | Do you hear what I tell you? |
| *Drinkwater* | 'In a very gentlemanly way.' |
| | |
| *Corbett* | (*approaching the bed*) Drinkwater! |
| *Drinkwater* | 'Wha' cheer, all the neighbours cry Who're yer going to meet, Bill? 'Ave yer bought the street, Bill—' |

[ 229 ]

at which point the gloom of the bedclothes was irradiated by pale stars. I had been cuffed, with a firmness that penetrated the blankets. I leapt up indignantly to find Corbett standing over me. 'What are you doing?' I demanded with more heat than discretion. He pointed out that it was rather what was I doing? There ensued an argument, which he was good enough sport not to close peremptorily. I said he had no right to box my ears. He said I had no right to make horrible noises at that time of night. I said it was mean of him not to give me any warning. He said he had given me several. I said I couldn't hear him. He said that wasn't his fault. He asked me if I was hurt. I said, yes, I was; then I said no, I wasn't. I said I was sorry, and he said he was. All ended well, but after that I always refused to be the person who went out of the room.

While I was at Hall's, King Edward VII, then Prince of Wales, came down to Oxford to open the new municipal buildings. The city was *en fête*, and in the evening the senior boys of the House were given leave to be out until eight o'clock. The police had been reinforced by special drafts from Reading, the authorities being apprehensive of some recrudescence of the old town-and-gown temper. In the thickest congestion at Carfax, some imbecile threw a lighted cracker under the horse of a mounted officer, and for a moment the terrified animal plunged into the crowd where we were standing. The rider, however, with superb horsemanship, kept control, and we escaped. As the evening wore on the fears of trouble proved not to be groundless, and a rag developed such as had not been known in the city within living memory. At the hour when we ought to have been on our way back to Banbury Road, our services had been pressed by a combative gang of undergraduates, with whom we were engaged in an arm-linked sweep of the High. Several of them were run in, but we were presumably too small to be noticed, and reached home about ten o'clock, feeling very grand, and that the honours that had been thrust upon us were much more than worth the reproofs with which we were greeted.

Another incident of a similar nature took place in Oxford during my schooldays. When the Duke of Marlborough married Miss Consuelo Vanderbilt, he invited a number of men from Christ Church to a ball at Blenheim. The Dean refused to let them go, and cutting down the rope of Old Tom they sent it in pieces to the Duke as decoration for his ball-room. They also organised a rabbit-hunt in the quad, painted the statues red, and finally bombarded the locked doors of the Dean's quarters. The ringleaders were sent down, and this was the only time I saw one of the traditional mock-funerals passing through the Oxford streets to the station. The cabs and cabmen were draped heavily in crape, the 'corpses' themselves sitting shrouded bolt-upright on the drivers' seats.

## XL

DURING my last year at school I had an unsettled, rather lost sort of feeling. I was not unhappy at Hall's. Indeed, he ran a House with as much sense and consideration as one could wish. The discipline under him was gentle but good. There was very little bullying at the High School; so little that one exception remains sharply etched on the memory. A boy named Scott was much given to religious exercise; in fact, he read the Bible out of class. He was rather an ungainly fellow, who used his stick at hockey like a scythe. A certain ——, who intimidated the smaller boys by sticking pins into them and other such attentions, made Scott his particular butt. His small victims supported him in their sycophantic way. One day, Scott was reading his Bible in the open playground shed. ——, accompanied by his jackals, approached his quarry. He jeered and used offensive names. Scott asked him to go away, whereupon —— knocked the Bible out of his hand. The jackals laughed like the little toadies they were. Scott glowered dumbly for a moment at ——, then dived at his waist, lifted him high in the air, and

[ 233 ]

flung him face downwards on the gravel. Never was a tyrant's power more summarily broken. From that day, —— was a public scorn, and Scott a public hero.

Hall had a fierce hatred for this most abominable of school abuses. He rightly thought that any master who tolerated any sign of it was not fitted for his job. I remember being deeply impressed when one evening he called us all together, and told us that at a well-known public school a small boy had just killed himself, being unable any longer to bear the ill-usage inflicted on him by the senior for whom he fagged. The morale of this matter has improved enormously even during the past generation, but a defence is still sometimes made of the revolting heresy that a certain amount of bullying is a necessary incident of a system calculated to turn out manly men.

My restlessness at Hall's was due to no specific cause, but to a feeling of general uncertainty about myself. I had seen so little of my Father since I was nine, that with Winchester Road closed I had a vague sense of being homeless. Moreover, Hall's boarders had always been regarded by the day-boys with a certain amount of open suspicion and secret envy, and I seemed suddenly to have changed sides. I was conscious that in Banbury Road I was looked upon as an interloper, and in the playground as a deserter. It was all nonsense, doubtless, but it made me uneasy. And then, seeing my Father in the holidays, I learnt definitely that it would not be possible for me to go to the University, or even to stay much longer at school. There was no heartbreak for me in this, but I suddenly realised that I should shortly be going out into the world, without having the least idea what it meant or what I wanted to do.

The influence of a school upon one's mind is an incalculable thing. To say that my own schooldays were the happiest time of my life, or anything like it, would be a flat absurdity. On the whole, they were an irksome ordeal from which, by dint of wilfulness, I managed to extract a considerable amount of pleasure. But as the years have gone by, it has appeared that there was more in it than that. My classes were dull, my masters with a few exceptions were dull, the school-life in general, apart from the sports, was dull. And of all the dull little boys who were the despair of harassed masters, none was duller than I. I do not think that from first to last I sat down to a single lesson with the smallest degree of interest. All that was bad, and it would be futile to invest it with romantic goodness. And yet, it had its alleviating, if negative, virtues. I suffered no brutalities, I was lucky in my friends, I enjoyed a good deal of freedom outside school hours, and I was taught a sound average code of decent behaviour. I think that, in boys' schools particularly, the general advance that has been made of recent years both in intellectual tone and social contacts had then hardly begun. And yet I am now sure that I was then learning much more than I realised, and this, if not under inspired, at least under responsible direction. I like to think that the school was pleased with the song that I recently wrote at its request—Frederic Austin made a stirring tune for it. They sing it now on speech-days, and although it may seem a solemn kind of ditty to them, it has at least an emotion that they too will some day know:

> Mother of learning, let us be
> Good scholars all in serving thee,
> Good fellows too;
> So teach us that our enterprise
> May be both merciful and wise
> In all we do.
>
> When Tudor sat upon the throne,
> That manners maketh man was known
> In Oxenford,
> And may the Oxford names we bear
> Be duly spoken everywhere
> For sweet accord.

And be it work, or be it play,
Let us remember every day
One golden rule—
That whoso keeps his honour bright
By sparing not his utmost might,
Honours the school.

Saint Giles, Saint Clement, and Saint John
Bless the beds that we lie on,
And bend our bows;
City of Oxford sons, awake,
Sing up to life, her beauty take,
And scorn her blows.

As for the University, I had no academic ambition
towards it whatever. Indeed, although I had lived
in Oxford for six years, I had but a very shadowy
notion of what they did there. But, to an Oxford
schoolboy, the undergraduates seemed to be exem-
plars of all things bright and beautiful, and I had
cherished quite uninstructed hopes of becoming one
of them. It is doubtful whether even if I had won
a scholarship, the family resources would have
allowed me to take it. I was, however, as likely to
win a scholarship as to eat a crocodile. I had once
gone so far as to be coached by a friend in the sixth,
R. S. Holliday, who played hockey with a sapling,
for a closed school scholarship, and had failed ex-
pectedly but miserably. It was the only bid I ever

made for learning's garlands, save for an entry in the Oxford Locals, when I secured an undistinguished pass.

In the Christmas holidays of 1896 my Father told me that he hoped through an acquaintance to obtain for me a Junior Clerkship in the Northern Assurance Company. I did not know what assurance meant, associating it dimly with cheek. I went back to school, and a fortnight later was called up to London to sit for the entrance examination. The following week my Father was informed that I had satisfied the examiners, who must have been very simple-minded, and that, subject to medical report, I should be appointed Junior Clerk at the Nottingham Branch of the Company. The doctor was also satisfied, and at half-term, February, 1897, I left school, my age being fifteen years and a half.

My Father took me up to Nottingham, found lodgings for me, and there left me. The salary was twenty pounds a year with prospects of annual rises. It was arranged that I should render an account to my Father of weekly expenditure, which I found a great bore. The first year I had to be subsidised from home. At Christmas, however, my clerical progress had been such that Head Office awarded me a fifteen pound rise instead of the usual ten. On thirty-five pounds, with the addition of a suit of clothes and

an occasional postal order for ten shillings—perhaps
five pounds' worth in the year—I kept myself until
the following Christmas brought a further advance.
But all this belongs to a later part of my story.